SABRINA GHAYOUR

BAZAAR

VIBRANT VEGETARIAN RECIPES

MITCHELL BEAZLEY

To my darling boys... my wonderfully funny, intelligent, kind and crazy nephews Cyrus, Darius, Kasra and Dastan. Thank you for always being my biggest and most fierce supporters, for each of your unique personalities and differing opinions that have given me much insight into both food and life, as well as your no-nonsense, blunt deliveries if ever I've gone wrong. Love you boys. This one is for you.

An Hachette UK Company
www.hachette.co.uk

First published in Great Britain in 2019 by Mitchell Beazley,
an imprint of Octopus Publishing Group Ltd
Carmelite House
50 Victoria Embankment
London EC4Y 0DZ
www.octopusbooks.co.uk

Text copyright © Sabrina Ghayour 2019
Photography copyright © Kris Kirkham 2019
Design and layout copyright © Octopus Publishing Group Ltd 2019

ISBN 978 1 78472 517 4

A CIP catalogue record for this book is available from the British Library.

Printed and bound in China

10 9 8 7 6 5 4 3 2 1

Publishing Director: Stephanie Jackson
Managing Editor: Sybella Stephens
Copy Editor: Salima Hirani
Creative Director: Jonathan Christie
Senior Designer: Jaz Bahra
Illustrator: Abigail Read
Photographer: Kris Kirkham
Food Stylist: Laura Field
Props Stylist: Agathe Gits
Senior Production Manager: Peter Hunt

Note on ingredients
Sea salt flakes should be used where stated; Sabrina cooks with Maldon sea salt flakes.
Always use genuine rose water – it should be alcohol-free.

BAZAAR

CONTENTS

INTRODUCTION

'Bazaar' is the ancient Persian word for 'market' and is shared by many other Eastern cultures. If I close my eyes, I imagine the old traditional markets of the Middle East in years gone by, which were loud, bustling places, filled with colourful produce of every shape and description. Unusual smells would fill the air. The senses would be seduced at every turn – sights and sounds distracted all those coming into the bazaar, luring them to the many stands to fulfil their various requirements. No matter which country I travel to, one of my greatest joys is visiting a good market – one that retains a focus on fresh and simple produce, untainted by modernity or the bells and whistles of trendy treats. There is always inspiration and a culinary education to be had in every local bazaar. Having long thought of myself as one of the world's most consummate carnivores, I never thought I would see the day when I put pen to paper to write a book of vegetarian recipes. Why? You may ask. Well, simply put, in many cultures, including my own, if there is no meat on the table, the meal is considered incomplete. Some cultures have endured war and famine where food, and especially meat, has been scarce. As times improve, meat often becomes the centrepiece of any feast, as a sign that life is good and you are doing well, which is a tradition still evident in many cultures. I know that whenever I cook a meatless feast for my family, I don't announce it in advance for fear of the unnecessary but hilarious panic it would cause!

Recently, I have noticed that more and more people are choosing to eat less meat. I have found that, as I get older, I simply don't seem able to enjoy meat in the excessive and voracious manner in which I used to, or digest it as easily. Having said that, I remain the world's safest bet for winner of the 'Least Likely To Turn Vegetarian' prize, so for me, this is a book that showcases and celebrates how wonderful and satisfying meals can be when they contain only fruits, vegetables, pulses, grains and dairy products – this is something that I myself can occasionally forget.

I have written this book with meat-eaters in mind, because I feel it is we who really need the most help and inspiration when it comes to preparing simple meals without meat, that have plenty of flavour and satisfy all at the table.

I have started teaching many vegetarian cookery classes lately and have noticed that the vast majority of my students are not actually vegetarians, but those who eat meat and fish. They come in search of ideas to help them deliver delicious meals at home without falling back on the same old repertoire. I love taking time off from eating meat, but have often been guilty of resorting to the usual suspects for sustenance... and while pasta, potatoes, bread, rice and mountains of cheese have their perks and frequently satisfy, eventually you do just crave vegetables. Their colours, freshness, depth of flavour and varied textures sustain the desire to stick to a meatless meal. I'm hoping this book provides inspiration to all those who need it – vegetarian and meat-eaters alike.

I created these recipes with a single aim: to deliver as much flavour as possible using few ingredients. The one thing I would like you to remember is that each recipe is merely a suggestion of ingredients – feel free to add whatever additions you like. Don't stress about ingredients you cannot find – if you are missing an ingredient or don't like something, just leave it out, because, after all, life is too short to sweat the small stuff. I hope you will embrace these recipes and make them your own. Food should always be a pleasure... my stomach (and my waistline) took great pleasure in perfecting these recipes for you, so take this book into your kitchens and enjoy.

Sabrina Ghayour

LIGHT BITES & SHARING PLATES

CARROT, HALLOUMI & DILL BALLS

Rarely do you see carrots fried, so here I've combined them with halloumi to make these crispy little balls – perfect with drinks or as part of a feast. Probably one of the best things to have ever happened to the humble carrot, if I'm honest.

vegetable oil, for frying

2 large carrots, peeled and
    coarsely grated

250g halloumi cheese, coarsely grated

1 large egg

1 small packet (about 30g) of dill,
    finely chopped

4 tablespoons plain flour

2 teaspoons cumin seeds

1 teaspoon paprika

Maldon sea salt flakes and freshly
    ground black pepper

salad leaves, to serve

MAKES 16–18

Pour enough vegetable oil into a large saucepan to fill to a depth of 5cm. Heat the oil over a medium-high heat and bring to frying temperature (add a pinch of the mixture: if it sizzles immediately, the oil is hot enough). Line a plate with a double layer of kitchen paper.

Put the grated carrot and halloumi, along with the remaining ingredients, into a mixing bowl and season well with black pepper and just a little salt. Now work the mixture with your hands to combine it well.

When the oil is ready for deep-frying, take roughly 1 tablespoon of the mixture and roll it into a ball that would fit perfectly into the tablespoon measure. Repeat with the remaining mixture. Carefully lower the balls into the hot oil and fry in batches for 2–3 minutes, until deep golden brown. Remove with a slotted spoon and transfer to the paper-lined plate to drain. Serve hot with salad leaves.

BROAD BEAN & RICOTTA DIP

Broad beans carry so many childhood memories for me. Arriving home from school on the rare occasion my Grandma was making one of the handful of dishes she learned to make in the 1980s, she would sit me in front of enormous bowls of broad beans with skins on and all she would say was, 'Peel them'. I remember the overpowering smell of the skins on my hands when we were done peeling, but it was worth the effort because the beans were so delicious. This broad bean and ricotta dip serves quite a few people, so it's perfect for sharing.

approximately 750g frozen (skin-on) or 400g peeled broad beans

2 fat garlic cloves, crushed

finely grated zest and juice of 1 unwaxed lemon

good drizzle of olive oil, plus a little extra to serve

500g ricotta cheese

2 teaspoons sumac

4 spring onions, very thinly sliced from root to tip

1 small packet (about 30g) of dill, finely chopped

Maldon sea salt flakes and freshly ground black pepper

toasted bread, to serve

SERVES 6–8

If using frozen skin-on broad beans, rinse them to remove any ice, then cook in boiling water for 5 minutes. Drain the beans in a sieve and rinse under cold running water to stop the cooking process and until cool enough to handle.

Peel each bean to remove the outer skins and place the peeled beans in the bowl of a food processor. Add the garlic, lemon zest and juice and olive oil to the bowl and pulse to grind down the mixture to a nice chunky texture, ensuring no large chunks remain.

Transfer the mixture to a large serving bowl. Add the ricotta, sumac, spring onions, dill, plenty of freshly milled black pepper and a good amount of salt. Mix well, then leave to stand for 5–10 minutes to allow the flavours to develop. Adjust the seasoning if necessary, then drizzle with extra olive oil and serve with toasted bread.

SUMAC, TOMATO & GARLIC TOASTS
WITH LABNEH

I'm obsessed with tomatoes on toast either in the Spanish style of pan con tomate or the Italian bruschetta. I used to make mini versions of these for clients as canapés, which proved so popular that I was asked to serve them as starters rather than finger food. The addition of sumac gives the tomatoes a citrusy note, and I never need an excuse to add coriander to tomatoes. They are incredibly moreish and I am happy to eat several of these as a meal by themselves; simple yet terribly good.

1 large ciabatta, cut into 12 slices

1 large or 2 small garlic cloves, peeled

4 large, ripe vine tomatoes,
    very finely chopped

½ small red onion, very finely chopped

2 teaspoons sumac, plus extra to garnish

½ small packet (about 15g) of fresh
    coriander, finely chopped (reserve
    some for garnish)

olive oil

4 heaped tablespoons labneh or thick
    Greek yogurt

Maldon sea salt flakes and freshly
    ground black pepper

MAKES 12

Chargrill the bread in a griddle pan on both sides or use a toaster. Lightly rub the surface of each slice with the raw garlic.

Mix the tomatoes, onion, sumac and coriander in a bowl. Add a little drizzle of olive oil and season well with salt and pepper.

Divide the tomato mixture between the toasts, spreading it across the surface of each piece. Top each with a teaspoon of labneh or yogurt and garnish each with a little pinch of sumac, the reserved coriander and a drizzle of olive oil. Serve immediately.

FETA & SPRING ONION-STUFFED POTATO SKINS

Nothing screams comfort to me more than creamy mashed potato, and this dish provides a delicious twist by combining it with another favourite of mine – the humble potato skin. Simple, delicious and quite filling – you can easily adapt the flavours to use up whatever other ingredients you have lurking in your fridge. It's also perfect for little hands, as kids love getting stuck into making these.

4 baking potatoes

50g butter

5–6 spring onions, thinly sliced from root to tip

200g feta cheese, crumbled

½ small packet (about 15g) of tarragon, leaves finely chopped

1 tablespoon garlic granules

1 teaspoon nigella seeds

Maldon sea salt flakes and freshly ground black pepper

SERVES 4–6

Preheat the oven to 220°C (200°C fan), Gas Mark 7.

Place the whole potatoes on a baking tray and bake for 25–30 minutes, then reduce the oven temperature to 200°C (180°C fan), Gas Mark 6, and cook for a further 1 hour, until the potatoes are cooked through. Remove from the oven.

Allow the potatoes to cool slightly, then cut each potato in half. Scoop out the flesh from each half into a bowl and set aside the skins.

Season the flesh generously with salt and pepper and add the butter to the bowl. Using a potato masher or a fork, roughly mash the butter, salt and pepper into the potato – don't worry if the mixture is not completely smooth. Use a spoon to stir in the spring onion, feta, tarragon, garlic granules and nigella seeds and mix well. Adjust the seasoning if desired.

Fill the potato skins with the mash mixture and pack the filling firmly into the skins. Set the stuffed skins on a baking tray and bake for 30 minutes, or until just starting to brown on top. Serve hot.

CHICKPEA & VEGETABLE KOFTAS

WITH TAHINI SAUCE

As someone already had the idea of inventing falafel wraps, I came up with this lighter version, which is absolutely delicious, packs in the vegetables and can easily be adapted to suit whatever you have in the fridge. With all the appeal of an indulgent kebab, these koftas are incredibly moreish on their own with a drizzle of tahini sauce on top.

2 x 400g cans chickpeas

3 fat garlic cloves, crushed

1 carrot, peeled and grated

1 sweet potato (about 300g), grated
    with the skin left on

1 small packet (about 30g) of fresh
    coriander, finely chopped (reserve
    a handful to serve)

4 spring onions, finely sliced

1 teaspoon turmeric

1 teaspoon ground cumin

1 teaspoon ground cinnamon

1 teaspoon chilli flakes

4 tablespoons chickpea (gram) flour

1 egg

generous amount of Maldon sea salt
    flakes and freshly ground black pepper

vegetable oil, for frying

For the tahini sauce

150g Greek yogurt

1 garlic clove, crushed

2 teaspoons ground coriander

3 tablespoons thick tahini

juice of ½ lemon

generous amount of Maldon sea salt
    flakes and freshly ground black pepper

To serve

6 tortilla wraps

few handfuls of rocket leaves

1 red onion, halved and thinly sliced

MAKES 18–20

Drain both cans of chickpeas, place the chickpeas into a large mixing bowl and use a potato masher or the end of a rolling pin to mash them. Add all the remaining kofta ingredients, except the oil, and using your hands pummel or pound (which is what the word 'kofta' means in Persian) into a sticky, even mixture. Refrigerate the mixture while you make the tahini sauce.

To make the tahini sauce, combine the ingredients in a jug. Add just enough warm water to loosen the mixture to a thick pouring cream consistency. Set aside.

Pour enough vegetable oil into a large, deep frying pan or saucepan to fill to a depth of about 2.5cm. Heat the oil over a medium-high heat and bring to frying temperature (add a pinch of the kofta mixture: if it sizzles immediately, the oil is hot enough). Line a tray with a double layer of kitchen paper.

When the oil is ready for frying, scoop up a rounded dessertspoonful of the kofta mixture and use the edges of the bowl to smooth it a little. Lower it carefully into the hot oil. Repeat with the remaining mixture, but do not overcrowd the pan – fry in batches to avoid reducing the temperature of the oil. Fry the koftas for a couple of minutes on each side, or until deep golden brown, then remove them from the pan using a slotted spoon and transfer to the paper-lined tray to drain.

Serve 3 koftas in each tortilla wrap with a good drizzle of the tahini sauce, some rocket leaves, some sliced red onion and a final flourish of the reserved coriander.

SPICED BUTTERMILK
FRIED TOMATOES

This is definitely one of my better ideas. When I made my mother try one, with her first bite she smiled and said, 'How on earth do you come up with this stuff?' Rest assured, this is her unique way of paying a compliment! My only advice is don't be tempted to use ripe tomatoes for this recipe – the firmer and more underripe, the better.

vegetable oil, for frying

200g best-quality polenta
    (not quick-cook)

250ml buttermilk

1 teaspoon cayenne pepper

2 teaspoons garlic granules

2 teaspoons sumac

4 large tomatoes, such as beef tomatoes

3 tablespoons dried wild oregano

Maldon sea salt flakes and freshly
    ground black pepper

SERVES 4-6

Pour enough vegetable oil into a large, deep frying pan or saucepan to fill to a depth of about 2.5cm. Heat the oil over a medium-high heat and bring to frying temperature (add a little polenta: if it sizzles immediately, the oil is hot enough). Line a plate with a double layer of kitchen paper.

Pour the polenta on to a plate and set aside. In a separate bowl, mix the buttermilk with the cayenne pepper, garlic granules, sumac and a generous amount of salt and pepper.

Slice the tomatoes into 1.5cm-thick slices – I usually get about 4 slices per tomato. Discard the ends, since the polenta doesn't stick to the skin very easily.

Drag a tomato slice through the buttermilk and shake off any excess liquid, then place it gently in the polenta and coat the cut sides and the edges as best you can, carefully patting the polenta on to the slice to encrust it. Lower it carefully into the hot oil, then repeat with the remaining tomato slices, frying in batches to avoid overcrowding the pan. Gently fry the slices for about 1 minute on each side, or until they start to brown. If they brown too fast, your oil is too hot, in which case switch off the heat and cook a few slices, then when the oil is at the right temperature, switch the heat back on.

Remove the slices from the oil with a slotted spoon and transfer to the paper-lined plate to drain, then sprinkle over some salt and the oregano. Serve the tomatoes hot.

CUCUMBER & FETA BRUSCHETTA

This is one of my favourite breakfasts. Sounds weird, but I am addicted to the combination of yogurt mixed with feta and topped with cucumber. It really does make the most satisfying snack, and the spices and pomegranate seeds take it to another level. They can also easily be made in smaller bites and served as finger food, too. Use half a regular cucumber thinly sliced into half moons if you can't find baby cucumbers.

200g feta cheese, finely crumbled

100g Greek yogurt

6 slices of sourdough bread

5–6 baby cucumbers, cut diagonally
   into 5mm-thick slices

1 teaspoon sumac

1 teaspoon dried wild oregano

1 teaspoon pul biber chilli flakes

½ teaspoon nigella seeds

50g pomegranate seeds

olive oil, for drizzling (optional)

Maldon sea salt flakes and freshly
   ground black pepper

SERVES 6

Combine the feta and yogurt in a bowl, and mash the mixture. Season with black pepper and just a little salt.

Chargrill the sourdough in a griddle pan on both sides or use a toaster.

Divide the feta mixture into 6 portions and spread a portion on to each slice of toast. Arrange the cucumber slices on top, then sprinkle over the sumac, oregano and pul biber.

Scatter over the nigella seeds and, lastly, the pomegranate seeds. Drizzle over a little olive oil, if desired, and serve immediately.

TURMERIC, SPINACH & SWEET POTATO FRITTERS

There are very few things that aren't improved by frying, and that includes vegetables – especially sweet potatoes. Turmeric is underrated as a spice, but I like it to be a main player in my cooking, just as long as it is not too overpowering and strikes the perfect balance with the other ingredients in a recipe. Eat these fritters with a few dipping sauces on the side – sweet chilli sauce is my personal favourite pairing.

300g sweet potato, peeled and
    coarsely grated
150g baby spinach leaves, finely chopped
3 teaspoons turmeric
1 teaspoon chilli flakes
3 large eggs
100g plain flour
1 teaspoon baking powder
vegetable oil, for frying
Maldon sea salt flakes and freshly ground
    black pepper
sweet chilli sauce, to serve

MAKES APPROXIMATELY 20

Put the sweet potato, spinach, turmeric, chilli flakes, eggs, flour and baking powder into a mixing bowl and mix well. Season generously with salt and pepper, then allow the batter to rest for 15 minutes.

Pour enough vegetable oil into a large, deep frying pan or saucepan to fill to a depth of about 5cm. Heat the oil over a medium-high heat and bring to frying temperature (add a pinch of mixture: if it sizzles immediately, the oil is hot enough). Line a plate with a double layer of kitchen paper.

When the oil is ready, stir the batter well. Using 2 dessertspoons, form quenelles of the mixture: scoop up the mixture with one spoon and use the other to press down and shape it. Lower the quenelles carefully into the hot oil and fry in batches, 6 at a time – it is important not to overcrowd the pan or the temperature of the oil will drop and your fritters will not be crisp. Fry the fritters for 1 minute, then turn them over and fry for another minute or so, or until nicely browned all over. Remove the fritters from the oil using a slotted spoon and transfer to the paper-lined plate to drain. Serve hot with sweet chilli sauce.

SPICED CRUDITÉ PLATTER

WITH TURMERIC & CUMIN HUMMUS

Sometimes we all need a little encouragement when it comes to consuming raw vegetables, and the simple spice treatment on this crudité platter transforms humble raw vegetables into something special, particularly when served with my chunky turmeric and cumin hummus. Persians like to snack on large quantities of seasoned baby cucumbers, but sprinkling them with a highly flavoursome spice blend takes raw veg to the next level – with minimum effort and to maximum effect. It's easy to eat half this platter in no time at all...

1 large cucumber, cut into batons

150g radishes, halved

4–5 celery sticks (with leaves), cut into 5cm batons

250g cherry or baby plum tomatoes

8 carrots, peeled and halved lengthways (or 4 large carrots, peeled and cut into batons)

olive oil, for drizzling

Maldon sea salt flakes and freshly ground black pepper

For the toasted-spice seasoning

1 teaspoon cumin seeds

1 teaspoon coriander seeds

1 teaspoon yellow mustard seeds

½ teaspoon chilli flakes

1 teaspoon dried wild oregano

For the turmeric & cumin hummus

2 x 400g cans chickpeas (reserve the liquid from 1 can, drain the second can)

12–15g fresh turmeric, peeled and finely grated

1 fat garlic clove, very finely chopped

2 teaspoons cumin seeds, toasted and crushed using a pestle and mortar

finely grated zest and juice of 1 unwaxed lemon

4 teaspoons tahini

olive oil, for drizzling

Maldon sea salt flakes and freshly ground black pepper

To make the toasted-spice seasoning, heat a small frying pan over a medium heat. Add the cumin, coriander and mustard seeds to the dry pan and toast them, shaking the pan, for 2 minutes. Transfer the toasted seeds to a pestle and mortar, mix in the chilli flakes and grind to a coarse powder. Stir in the oregano, then set aside.

To make the turmeric and cumin hummus, use a food processor or blender to blitz 1 can of chickpeas with its canning liquid until completely smooth. Add a generous amount of salt and pepper, the fresh turmeric, garlic, crushed cumin seeds, lemon zest and juice and tahini and blitz again briefly until the ingredients are all well incorporated.

Add the remaining can of drained chickpeas and pulse briefly to break them down slightly. I like a nice chunky texture, but if you prefer a smooth hummus, continue to blitz until the mixture is smooth. Check and adjust the seasoning, adding salt and pepper as necessary. Transfer the hummus to a serving bowl and drizzle over some olive oil.

Arrange the prepared vegetables attractively on a serving platter (place the cucumber batons skin-side down). Drizzle over a good amount of olive oil, season generously with salt and pepper, then season heavily with the toasted-spice seasoning. Serve immediately with the hummus.

SERVES 6–8

POTATO CRISPS
WITH SPICED SALT & LIME

I have a life-long obsession with crisps. Over the years I have become something of a self-styled crisp aficionado, pairing crisps with different cheeses and cured meats (because that's all you have the energy to eat after a 17-hour shift cooking food for others), so I like to think I'm now a bit of a connoisseur. This is a spectacular treatment for the humble crisp, but to be perfectly honest, you can use a shop-bought packet of good-quality, hand-cooked plain potato crisps. However, nothing beats the flavour of homemade crisps – these are very much worth the effort.

4 potatoes (unpeeled)

1 tablespoon fine sea salt

about 1 litre vegetable or sunflower oil, for deep-frying

2 limes, cut into wedges, to serve

For the spiced salt

2 tablespoons Maldon sea salt flakes or 1 tablespoon fine salt

½ teaspoon chilli powder

½ teaspoon ground coriander

½ teaspoon dried wild oregano

½ teaspoon sumac

SERVES 6-8

Using a mandoline slicer or a food processor slicing attachment set to a medium thickness, thinly slice the potatoes – aim for the thickness of a matchstick. Alternatively, thinly slice by hand. Rinse the slices to remove any excess starch, then leave them to soak for about 20 minutes in a large mixing bowl filled with cold water and the fine sea salt.

Meanwhile, using a pestle and mortar, grind the spiced salt ingredients together. Set aside.

Once the soaking time has elapsed, drain the potato slices, rinse them, then dry them as well as you can with a clean tea towel or kitchen paper.

Pour enough vegetable or sunflower oil into a large, deep frying pan or saucepan to fill to a depth of about 7cm. Alternatively heat a deep-fat fryer. Heat the oil over a medium-high heat and bring to frying temperature (add a potato slice: if it sizzles immediately, the oil is hot enough). Line a large tray with a double layer of kitchen paper.

You'll need to fry the potato slices in batches, depending on the size of your pan. Carefully lower the first batch of potato slices into the hot oil stir gently with a slotted spoon to avoid them sticking together and fry for a few minutes, or until golden brown. Remove the cooked crisps from the hot oil using a slotted spoon and transfer to the paper-lined plate to drain. Repeat with the remaining batches of potato slices.

To serve, place the crisps on a board or flat platter and season with the spiced salt as desired. Serve with the lime wedges for squeezing over just before eating.

TURMERIC, LEMON & VODKA COOLERS

Herbs, aromatics, spices and even vegetables can provide a base for some interesting tipples. If there is a cocktail with turmeric in it on a bar menu, it's virtually a given that I will be ordering it. My love for turmeric runs so deep that I came up with this blend inspired by the hot drink I make when I need a natural remedy to fight a cold. Although I must admit, I much prefer this medicine in cocktail form!

ice cubes or crushed ice

300–400ml vodka (use 50ml per
    cocktail)

lemon slices, to garnish (optional)

For the turmeric syrup

750ml boiling water

1 unwaxed lemon, rind peeled into strips,
    plus the juice

30g fresh turmeric, peeled and cut into
    rough chunks

200g golden caster sugar

MAKES 6–8

First make the syrup. Heat a small saucepan over a low heat. Pour in the measured boiling water, then add the strips of lemon rind, the lemon juice, turmeric chunks and the sugar and stir briefly until the sugar dissolves. Allow the mixture to cook very gently – do not let it simmer or bubble to avoid any liquid evaporating. After 20 minutes, remove the pan from heat, stir the contents, then leave to cool completely.

Fill a Highball glass two-thirds full with ice cubes or crushed ice and add 100ml of the cooled turmeric syrup, followed by 50ml vodka. Stir, then add more ice, garnish with a lemon slice, if desired, and serve immediately. Repeat with the remaining turmeric syrup and vodka.

Top left: Barberry Martinis;
Top right: Ginger, Honey & Lime Margaritas
Centre: Turmeric, Lemon & Vodka Coolers

GINGER, HONEY & LIME MARGARITAS

Tequila gets such a bad rap, perhaps because many of us have some sort of tequila story that didn't end well... I have a love for good tequila, and classic Margaritas are a favourite of mine. I love lime in pretty much every cocktail, but it's the ginger and honey that make this drink so spectacular, therefore this recipe comes with a warning: you may find yourself making many of these – they are just too good!

50ml white tequila

juice of 1 lime

2.5cm piece of fresh root ginger, peeled and grated

1 tablespoon clear honey

ice cubes

MAKES 1

Pour the tequila into a tumbler (or cocktail shaker), add the lime juice, ginger and honey and stir the mixture well to ensure the honey dissolves. Once the honey has dissolved, add ice and stir using a chopstick or similar (or shake if using a cocktail shaker) until chilled, then strain the drink into a Margarita glass and serve.

BARBERRY MARTINIS

Some would argue that drinks are every bit as important as the food at a good meal. I must confess that I have never placed great importance on liquid refreshment, instead always throwing myself into producing really good food. But for me, a good cocktail relies on a few factors: sweet, sour, cold and refreshing. This barberry Martini (or Bar-tini!) does the job beautifully.

500ml boiling water

75g dried barberries

4 tablespoons clear honey

200ml vodka

8–10 ice cubes

MAKES 8

Pour the measured boiling water over the barberries and leave to infuse until the liquid has cooled completely. Blitz the mixture using a high powered blender until completely smooth. Strain the liquid into a jug, then add honey and stir until dissolved.

Add the vodka, which should take the volume of liquid to approximately 800ml. Pour half this mixture into a cocktail shaker, add half the ice cubes and shake until cold. Strain into 4 Martini glasses. Repeat with remaining mixture and ice cubes.

EGGS & DAIRY

GRILLED HALLOUMI FLATBREADS
WITH PRESERVED LEMON & BARBERRY SALSA

This is my version of a taco, but with all the punch and vibrancy you would associate with Middle Eastern flavours. You can substitute the halloumi for Indian paneer or tofu. The flatbreads alone are incredibly moreish – you may never buy shop-bought flatbreads again!

2 x 250g blocks halloumi cheese

2 tablespoons Greek-style yogurt

5cm piece of fresh turmeric, peeled and finely grated

1 garlic clove, crushed

finely grated zest of 1 unwaxed lime

good squeeze of lime juice

vegetable oil

1 x recipe 'Shaken' Sweet Quick Pickled Onions (see page 193)

pul biber chilli flakes, to garnish

Maldon sea salt flakes and black pepper

For the flatbreads

30g unsalted butter, melted

175g plain flour

100ml semi-skimmed milk

2 teaspoons freshly ground black pepper

2 teaspoons garlic granules

1 tablespoon olive oil

For the salsa

½ small packet (about 15g) of fresh dill, roughly chopped

4 preserved lemons, deseeded and very finely chopped

1 tablespoon dried barberries

1 avocado, peeled, stoned and roughly diced

2 teaspoons nigella seeds

For the harissa yogurt

250g Greek-style yogurt

1 heaped tablespoon rose harissa

MAKES 4

Cut each block of halloumi into 4 thick, equal slices. Put the yogurt, grated turmeric, crushed garlic and lime zest into a bowl, add the lime juice and mix well. Season with salt and pepper. Leave the halloumi slices to marinate while you're making the flatbreads.

Put all the flatbread ingredients, except the oil, into a mixing bowl and mix until a firm dough has formed. Wrap the dough in clingfilm and leave to rest at room temperature for 30 minutes.

To make the salsa, mix the ingredients together in a small bowl, season with salt and pepper and set aside.

To make the harissa yoghurt, mix the ingredients together in another bowl, season with salt and pepper, and chill until ready to serve.

When you're ready to cook the flatbreads, preheat a large frying pan over a medium heat. Divide the dough into 4 equal portions and roll out each piece into a thin round, about 25cm in diameter. Brush the hot pan with olive oil and cook the flatbreads, one at a time, for about 45–60 seconds on each side, or until lightly browned.

In the same frying pan, heat a drizzle of vegetable oil over a medium-high heat. Add the marinated halloumi slices and fry for about 1 minute on each side, or until nicely browned.

Divide the halloumi between the flatbreads and dollop a generous amount of the harissa yogurt on top. Add the salsa and some pickled onions, then sprinkle over some pul biber. Roll up and serve immediately.

BAKED HALLOUMI

I cannot exist without halloumi in my refrigerator at all times, and for good reason: it can make a meal in minutes. The more of it I eat, the more of it I crave, so I like to come up with different ways of using it. I think I've cracked it with this spicy, salty and sweet combo, which is ridiculously simple to make and perfect for tearing into with friends – or, if you are greedy like me, eating alone.

250g block of halloumi cheese

2 tablespoons rose harissa

2 tablespoons clear honey

juice of ½ lime

bread, to serve

SERVES 1–4

Preheat the oven to 220ºC (200ºC fan), Gas Mark 7.

Take a large square of kitchen foil and line it with baking paper. Place the block of halloumi on it in the centre of this double layer.

Mix the harissa, honey and lime juice together in a small jug or bowl. Pour the mixture over the halloumi. Draw up the baking paper around and over the block, then repeat with the foil and seal the parcel tightly at the top. Place on a baking tray and bake for 30 minutes, then serve immediately with bread.

SPICED BEAN SCOTCH EGGS

*Scotch eggs are a thing of beauty and are equally good eaten hot or cold. I felt compelled
to come up with a version that packs in plenty of flavour but without the meat.
All you need to decide is whether you prefer a soft, oozy yolk or a hard-boiled egg centre.*

2 x 400g cans kidney beans, drained
and rinsed

2 teaspoons turmeric

2 teaspoons ground ginger

2 teaspoons ground cinnamon

2 teaspoons pul biber chilli flakes

2 carrots, peeled and coarsely grated

1 onion, grated (drain and discard
the juice)

1 small packet (about 15g) of dill,
very finely chopped

8 eggs

2 tablespoons plain flour, for dusting

100–125g fine white breadcrumbs

vegetable oil, for frying

Maldon sea salt flakes and freshly
ground black pepper

MAKES 6

Put the beans and spices into a large mixing bowl, add a generous amount
of salt and pepper and mash until the mixture is as smooth as possible.
Add the carrot, onion and dill and mix well using your hands. Refrigerate
the mixture until needed.

Pour boiling water from a kettle into a saucepan set over a medium-high
heat. Once the water is bubbling, carefully lower in 6 of the eggs and boil
for 5 minutes if you like them soft-boiled, or 7 minutes for hard-boiled.
Drain the eggs and place them under cold running water to arrest the
cooking process. Once cooled, carefully tap all around the eggshells with
a teaspoon and gently peel away the shell, taking care not to break the egg.

Put the flour and breadcrumbs into separate bowls. Crack the remaining
2 eggs into a shallow bowl and beat together. Remove the bean mixture
from the refrigerator and divide it into 6 equal portions (I weigh the
mixture to help divide it equally). Flatten one portion into a patty shape.
Gently dust the exterior of an egg with flour, then place it into the centre
of the bean mixture patty and close up the mixture around the egg until
it is sealed and smooth. Roll the coated egg first in beaten egg, then in the
breadcrumbs, taking time to pat them well into the bean mixture. Repeat
with the remaining eggs and portions of bean mixture. Freeze the eggs for
about 20 minutes, which helps them retain their shape during frying.

Pour enough vegetable oil into a large, deep frying pan or saucepan to fill
to a depth of about 7cm, or alternatively heat a deep-fat fryer. Heat the
oil over a medium-high heat and bring to frying temperature (add a pinch
of the breadcrumb mixture: if it sizzles immediately, the oil is ready).
Line a plate with a double layer of kitchen paper. When the oil is hot,
remove the eggs from the freezer. Cook the eggs 2 at a time in the hot oil
for 2–3 minutes, or until deeply golden brown all over. Remove the eggs
from the oil with a slotted spoon and transfer them to the paper-lined
plate to drain. Sprinkle over some salt flakes and serve warm.

AUBERGINE & CARAMELIZED ONION KUKU

Iranians are big fans of kuku, which is essentially a frittata. We have four classic versions, and one of them uses aubergines. Naturally, I have added my own twist in the form of caramelized onions and a little parsley. If you want to make this more of a meal, add feta cheese and serve it with bread.

generous pinch of best-quality saffron threads, ground to a powder using a pestle and mortar

3 tablespoons boiling water

vegetable oil, for frying

4 large aubergines, cut into 2.5cm cubes

3 large onions, halved and thinly sliced into half moons

10 large eggs

2 tablespoons thick Greek yogurt

2 tablespoons plain flour

2 teaspoons baking powder

1 small packet (about 30g) of flat leaf parsley, finely chopped

Maldon sea salt flakes and freshly ground black pepper

SERVES 10

Put the saffron powder into a small cup and pour over the boiling water. Leave to steep until the liquid is cool.

Line 2 trays with a double layer of kitchen paper. Pour enough vegetable oil into a large saucepan to fill to a depth of about 2.5cm. Heat the oil over a medium-high heat, then add half the aubergine cubes. Fry for a few minutes, without stirring, until brown and cooked through (remove a piece and mash it with a fork – there should be no resistance). Remove the aubergine from the pan using a slotted spoon and transfer to one of the paper-lined trays to drain. Add a layer of kitchen paper on top of the aubergine to absorb the excess oil. Repeat the process with the remaining aubergine, topping up the oil in the pan as necessary. Set the cooked aubergine aside and leave to cool.

Heat another large saucepan over a medium heat and drizzle in enough oil to coat the base of the pan. Once hot, add the onion and cook for 30 minutes or so, stirring regularly, until soft and cooked through but without blackening. This process requires a little patience, but the flavour will be worthwhile. Remove the onion from the pan using a slotted spoon and transfer to the other paper-lined tray to drain. Leave to cool.

Preheat the oven to 200°C (180°C fan), Gas Mark 6. Select a large baking tray or ovenproof dish, about 26 x 20cm and line it with baking paper.

Crack the eggs into a large mixing bowl and whisk. Add the saffron solution, yogurt, flour and baking powder and mix well. Stir in the cooled onion and aubergine and the parsley, then season generously with salt and pepper and mix well. Pour the mixture into the prepared baking tray or dish and ensure the ingredients are evenly distributed across it. Bake for 30 minutes (check after 25), or until the top is golden and beginning to brown, and a knife inserted into the centre comes out clean of raw egg. Allow to cool slightly, then cut it into slices. Serve with mixed salad leaves.

LIME & ALLSPICE PANEER
WITH MANGO CHILLI SALSA

What I love about Indian paneer is that it doesn't melt too easily, so is the perfect carrier for marinades and spice rubs. I've turned to allspice for this recipe – it's an underused and somewhat misunderstood spice. It was thought to have multiple flavour profiles akin to a blend of many (or 'all') spices, which is how it got its name – as a total spice nerd, this sort of trivia fascinates me! The flavour works beautifully with the paneer and the lovely mango salsa.

250g paneer, cut into 12 equal cubes

For the marinade
finely grated zest of 1 unwaxed lime
1 teaspoon allspice berries, finely ground
  using a pestle and mortar
1 teaspoon garlic granules
2 tablespoons olive oil
1 teaspoon dried wild thyme
generous amount of Maldon sea
  salt flakes

For the mango chilli salsa
1 teaspoon black mustard seeds
1 teaspoon coriander seeds
1 ripe mango, peeled, stoned and
  finely diced
1 long red chilli, deseeded and
  finely chopped
½ red onion, very finely chopped
juice of ½ lime
1 tablespoon olive oil
½ small packet (about 15g) of fresh
  coriander, finely chopped
Maldon sea salt flakes and freshly
  ground black pepper

SERVES 2–4

Combine the ingredients for the marinade in a small bowl.

Put the paneer cubes into a food bag and pour in the marinade. Seal the bag, then rub the marinade really well over the cubes to coat them. Set aside for 30 minutes to marinate.

Meanwhile, make the mango chilli salsa. Toast the mustard seeds and coriander seeds in a dry frying pan over a medium heat for 2 minutes, or until they release their aroma. Remove from the heat, then crush using a pestle and mortar.

Put the remaining salsa ingredients into a serving bowl, add the crushed seeds and mix well. Season to taste, then set aside.

Heat a large saucepan over a medium heat. Add the paneer, along with the marinade, and fry for about 1 minute on each side, or until nicely browned. Serve immediately, with the mango salsa dotted on top.

POM-BOMBE

I first made this as an alternative to a Christmas cheese board, but, quite frankly, it works all year round as a visually spectacular addition to any table. It does require a degree of patience to stud the cheese ball with pomegranate seeds, but it is well worth the effort – and it can be made the day before and kept refrigerated until ready to serve. You can also make it as big as you like by doubling or tripling the recipe quantities. Serve it with crispbreads, crackers, mini toasts and even chicory leaves.

350g soft goats' cheese (chèvre with the rind cut off also works)

2 heaped teaspoons sumac

15g chives, snipped or thinly sliced

finely grated zest of 1 unwaxed orange

1–2 teaspoons pul biber chilli flakes

200g pomegranate seeds

50g pistachio nut slivers or 75g roughly chopped whole pistachio nuts

freshly ground black pepper

SERVES 4–6

Mix the cheese, sumac, chives, orange zest, pul biber and a generous seasoning of pepper in a mixing bowl until evenly combined.

Lay a large sheet of clingfilm on your work surface. Using a spatula, scrape the cheese mixture out of the bowl and into the centre of the clingfilm. Gather the 4 corners of the clingfilm together, expel any air and twist the clingfilm just above the top of the ball to secure the cheese mixture. Use your hands to form the mixture inside the clingfilm into a ball. Refrigerate for 30 minutes or, preferably, freeze for about 10 minutes.

Remove the ball from the refrigerator or freezer, discard the clingfilm and place the ball on a serving plate. Stud the surface of the ball all over with the pomegranate seeds. Scatter the pistachios on top and around the base, studding the ball with a few pieces wherever you can. Cover with clingfilm and refrigerate until ready to serve.

KALE & CABBAGE KUKU
WITH PINE NUTS

Cabbage is so underrated. I use cabbage in so many ways – from salads, rice and pasta to pies, stir-fries and so much more. This is a delicious take on the most classic of all the Persian kuku (frittata) recipes, and the best news is you can use any type of cabbage or kale you can get your hands on.

vegetable oil

2 red onions, halved and thinly sliced into half moons

200g curly kale, tough stalks discarded, finely chopped

200g cabbage greens, cut into thin ribbons and roughly chopped

2 teaspoons garlic granules

1 heaped teaspoon ground fenugreek

1 heaped teaspoon turmeric

8 large eggs

2 teaspoons baking powder

2 tablespoons plain flour

2 tablespoons thick Greek yogurt

2 generous handfuls of dried barberries

40g pine nuts

200g feta cheese, little chunks no larger than 1cm picked off by hand

Maldon sea salt flakes and freshly ground black pepper

SERVES 4–6

Heat a large saucepan over a medium heat. Pour in enough vegetable oil to coat the base of the pan and allow it to heat up, then add the onion and fry gently for a few minutes, stirring from time to time, until soft and cooked through.

Increase the heat to medium-high and add the kale. Stir-fry for 2 minutes, or until completely softened and cooked through. Add the cabbage greens and stir-fry for 5–6 minutes, then add the garlic granules and spices, season generously with salt and pepper and mix well. Cook until the cabbage is wilted and cooked through. (You are not looking to retain the texture or keep the greens al dente for this dish.) Once cooked, take the pan off the heat and leave to cool a little.

Preheat the oven to 200°C (180°C fan), Gas Mark 6. Line a 16 x 30cm ovenproof dish with baking paper.

Crack the eggs into a large mixing bowl and whisk. Add the baking powder, flour, yogurt and also a little salt, if desired, and mix well. Add the barberries and pine nuts and, once the greens have cooled slightly, incorporate them into the egg mixture a little at a time, mixing well between each addition. Lastly, gently fold in the feta pieces. Pour the mixture into the prepared dish and use a spatula to ensure the ingredients are evenly distributed across the dish. Bake for 30 minutes (check after 25 minutes), or until the top is golden and beginning to brown and a knife inserted into the centre comes out clean of raw egg. Allow to cool slightly, then cut it into slabs to serve.

WORLD'S BEST TOASTIE

When I first threw these ingredients together after a bit of a fridge forage, I didn't have much faith that the result would turn out so well. I have to say, this halloumi, honey, harissa and tomato toastie with a pickled onion tang will satisfy cravings you didn't even know you had! Salty, sweet, juicy and spicy... the perfect way to start (or end) a day.

250g block of halloumi cheese, cut into 6 equal slices

olive oil

4 slices of good-quality bread

2 teaspoons rose harissa (it's powerful stuff, so use moderately, unless you like some heat)

2 tablespoons clear honey

2 tomatoes, sliced

2 tablespoons 'Shaken' Sweet Quick-Pickled Onions (*see* page 193)

40g butter

Maldon sea salt flakes and freshly ground black pepper

SERVES 2

Heat a frying pan over a medium heat, drizzle in a little olive oil and add the halloumi slices. Fry for about 2 minutes on each side, or until golden and crusted. Meanwhile, very lightly toast your bread slices on a low setting so that they are barely browned.

Remove the fried halloumi slices to a side plate. Use kitchen paper to wipe the pan clean.

Make a sandwich – place a slice of bread on your work surface, then lay half the halloumi slices across it. Smear half the rose harissa over the halloumi slices. Drizzle over half the honey. Now lay half the tomato slices across, top with some pickled onions and season well with black pepper and a little pinch of salt (bear in mind that the halloumi is already quite salty). Top with another slice of bread and press down on the sandwich. Repeat with the remaining ingredients.

At this point, you can brush the outsides with the melted butter and cook in a toasted sandwich maker if you have one. Alternatively, add one-quarter of the butter to the pan and let it melt over a medium heat, but don't let it burn (take the pan off the heat if sizzles too much). Transfer one of the sandwiches to the pan. Press the toastie by placing a small saucepan on top of the sandwich with a heavy weight, such as a can, inside. Cook over a medium heat for around 2 minutes, then check to see if the bread has browned. If so, lift up the sandwich using a fish slice, add one-third of the remaining butter, carefully turn over the sandwich and fry the other side until browned. Take the sandwich out of the pan and repeat the process with the remaining sandwich, then serve.

SOUPS & BOWL COMFORT

CARROT, FENNEL SEED & RED LENTIL SOUP

WITH LABNEH & SESAME OIL

I admit, I'm fussy when it comes to soups. A soup should be more than just warming – I like layers of flavour and different textures. It's easy to dismiss soups as simple or easy food, when in fact the best ones are put together with some thought. Having said that, good soup needn't be complicated, expensive or time-consuming; I believe the best things in life come together with the greatest of ease. This soup is easy to make and hits all the spots you didn't even know you had.

2 teaspoons fennel seeds

vegetable oil or ghee

50g fresh root ginger, peeled and finely chopped or grated

1 onion, diced

500g carrots, scrubbed and cut into rough chunks

2 fat garlic cloves, roughly chopped

1 teaspoon turmeric

2 litres boiling water

juice of ½ lemon (about 2 tablespoons)

150g uncooked red lentils

4 tablespoons labneh or thick Greek yogurt

4 teaspoons sesame oil

Maldon sea salt flakes and freshly ground black pepper

couple of pinches of pul biber chilli flakes, to garnish

SERVES 4

Toast the fennel seeds in a large, dry saucepan over a medium heat for 2 minutes, then drizzle in a little vegetable oil or ghee and add the ginger and onion. Sauté until the onion begins to soften, without letting it brown. Add the carrot to the pan and stir-fry until the edges begin to soften.

Now add the garlic, turmeric and a generous amount of salt and pepper to the saucepan and mix well. Pour over the boiling water, adjust the heat to bring the mixture to a simmer and simmer gently, without a lid, for 45 minutes. Allow to cool slightly, then blitz the mixture using a hand-held blender or transfer to a food processor or blender. Return the soup to the pan if necessary, adjust the seasoning, then stir in the lemon juice.

Set the pan over a medium heat and stir in the red lentils. Simmer, stirring occasionally, for 30–40 minutes, or until the lentils are soft. If the soup seems too thick, blitz half the mixture using the hand-held blender, food processor or blender.

Divide the soup between 4 bowls. Dollop 1 tablespoon of labneh into each bowl and drizzle 1 teaspoon of sesame oil over the top. Finish with a sprinkling of pul biber and serve.

SWEET POTATO & LIME SOUP

I love sweet potatoes in any way, shape or form. There is something addictive about their sweet and pleasingly digestible nature which I find genuinely comforting. In this delicious soup, their sweetness is balanced beautifully with fresh lime – and a crumble of feta on top makes it more of a meal.

olive oil

2 large onions, roughly diced

2kg sweet potatoes, peeled and
   cut into rough chunks

2 fat garlic cloves, peeled

1 teaspoon dried wild oregano

1 teaspoon chilli flakes, plus extra
   to garnish

1 teaspoon turmeric

1 litre boiling water

finely grated zest of 2 unwaxed limes
   and juice of 1

Maldon sea salt flakes and freshly
   ground black pepper

200g feta cheese, crumbled, to serve

SERVES 4–6

Place a large saucepan over a medium heat. Pour in enough olive oil to coat the base of the pan. Add the onion and cook for a few minutes until softened and translucent, without browning.

Mix the sweet potato chunks and garlic cloves into the saucepan and cook for 5–6 minutes, or until the edges begin to soften, without colouring.

Stir in the oregano and the spices, then pour in the boiling water. Mix well, cover the pan with a lid, reduce the heat to medium-low and simmer gently for 30 minutes, or until the sweet potato is cooked through.

Transfer the mixture to a food processor or blender and blitz. If the soup seems too thick, add boiling water, a little at a time, until you reach your desired consistency.

Return the soup to the saucepan and mix in the lime zest and juice. Season to taste, then cook for a further 15 minutes over a medium-low heat.

Serve with the crumbled feta on top, a drizzle of olive oil and extra chilli flakes, if desired.

RICE & VEGETABLE AASH
WITH PUY LENTILS

To say that aash is merely a soup would be underselling it – this hearty staple of Persian cuisine is much more than that. Always herb-based, there are many varieties: some with meat, some without, some with barley, rice, tomato or pomegranate molasses... all equally delicious. Aash is the best comfort food on a cold day, and virtuous enough to be the perfect meal all year round. This is my Western version, but it is still every bit as delicious.

olive oil, for frying

2 large white onions, finely chopped

100g flat leaf parsley, finely chopped

100g fresh coriander, finely chopped

5 large garlic cloves, crushed

3 teaspoons unsweetened tamarind paste

2 teaspoons paprika

3 tablespoons tomato purée

75g butter

1 heaped tablespoon plain flour

1 litre vegetable stock

1 litre cold water

100g basmati rice

100g uncooked Puy lentils

Maldon sea salt flakes and freshly
    ground black pepper

To garnish

1 small packet (about 30g) of dill,
    finely chopped

1 bunch of spring onions, thinly sliced

SERVES 6–8

Place a large saucepan over a medium heat. Pour in enough olive oil to coat the base of the pan. Add the onion and cook for a few minutes until softened and translucent, without browning.

Add the fresh herbs and cook them down for a few minutes until they are completely wilted and resemble cooked spinach. Stir in the garlic and cook for a few more minutes until soft and translucent without browning.

Mix the tamarind, paprika, tomato purée and butter into the pan, stir everything together well, then add the flour and mix well. Fry for a few minutes, then pour in the stock and the cold water, and season with a generous amount of salt and pepper.

Bring the contents of the saucepan to a rolling boil, then stir in the rice and Puy lentils. Reduce the heat and simmer, without a lid, for 25–30 minutes, or until the rice and lentils are cooked. If the soup seems too thick, add boiling water (up to 300ml), a little at a time, until you reach your desired consistency. Taste and adjust the seasoning as desired, then serve immediately (it will continue to absorb more liquid if left to sit), with the dill and sliced spring onions scattered on top.

SWEETCORN, POTATO & CHEDDAR CHOWDER

This is truly comfort in a bowl for a girl like me. Corn, potatoes and cheese together? Seriously – what's not to love? Creamy, slightly thick and utterly satisfying, gentle spicing gives this soup a little extra oomph. This is a full meal in a bowl, so you really won't need anything else.

olive oil

1 onion, finely chopped

1 teaspoon cumin seeds

kernels sliced from 2 sweetcorn cobs

3 garlic cloves, bashed

1 teaspoon turmeric

25g butter

350g potato, peeled and coarsely grated

1 litre boiling water

150g mature Cheddar cheese, grated

crème fraîche, to serve

Maldon sea salt flakes and freshly ground black pepper

SERVES 4–6

Place a large saucepan over a medium heat. Pour in enough olive oil to coat the base of the pan. Add the onion and cook for a few minutes until softened and translucent, without browning.

Stir in the cumin seeds and fry for 2 minutes, then add the sweetcorn, garlic and turmeric, and cook for a few minutes until softened.

Stir the butter and grated potato into the saucepan, season with salt and pepper and cook for 6–8 minutes, stirring regularly, or until the potato softens.

Pour in the boiling water, reduce the heat to low and simmer, without a lid, for 30 minutes, until the potato is cooked through. Stir in the cheese and allow it to melt, then ladle into bowls. Top each with a tablespoon of crème fraîche, a drizzle of olive oil and a grinding of black pepper, then serve immediately.

ZA'ATAR, LEEK & CELERIAC SOUP

I love celeriac, but sometimes it needs a few extra ingredients to give it a boost. I have always found that adding za'atar to a dish only improves matters further. This is an easy soup to throw together and it delivers on flavour in a big way.

olive oil, for frying

500g leeks, trimmed, cleaned and roughly chopped

800–900g celeriac, peeled and diced

3 fat garlic cloves, sliced

2 litres boiling water

50g butter

2 tablespoons Za'atar Blend (*see page 86*)

Maldon sea salt flakes and freshly ground black pepper

SERVES 4–6

Heat a large saucepan over a medium heat. Drizzle in a little olive oil, add the leek and cook for a few minutes, or until softened, without browning.

Stir in the celeriac and garlic and season with pepper and a good amount of salt. Cook for a further 12–15 minutes, or until the vegetables are softened. Do not allow the vegetables to brown, as you want to keep this soup white in colour. Pour in the boiling water, stir well, then reduce the heat to low and simmer, without a lid, for 30–40 minutes, or until the celeriac is soft.

Transfer the mixture to a food processor or blender and blitz. Return the soup to the saucepan, stir in the butter until melted, then serve in bowls garnished with the za'atar and a drizzle of olive oil.

ROASTED TOMATO
& CHILLI SOUP

*Roasting tomatoes really does intensify their flavour. If you dare, charring the edges a little improves them
even more. This is one of those dishes I would recommend you double up on so that you can freeze half
and gorge on it another day. Simple, full-flavoured and ever so comforting.*

1kg plum tomatoes, halved

2 long red chillies, halved lengthways
and deseeded

4 fat garlic cloves (unpeeled), wrapped
in a piece of kitchen foil to protect
them from burning

2 teaspoons cumin seeds

olive oil

2 slices of stale bread (I use sourdough),
cut into cubes

2–3 tablespoons Sabzi Sauce
(*see* page 195)

500ml boiling water

1 tablespoon red wine vinegar

1 heaped teaspoon caster sugar

Maldon sea salt flakes and freshly
ground black pepper

SERVES 2–4

Preheat the oven to 190°C (170°C fan), Gas Mark 5. Line the largest baking
tray you have with baking paper.

Lay the tomatoes in the prepared tray with the cut sides facing up. Add to the
tray the chillies and the garlic cloves in their foil. Season the tomatoes with
pepper and sprinkle the cumin seeds over them. Drizzle over a generous
amount of olive oil to ensure everything is coated. Roast for 45 minutes, or
until the tomatoes are very soft and slightly charred. Remove from oven and
leave to cool.

Heat a large saucepan over a medium-high heat and drizzle in 2–3 tablespoons
olive oil. Add the bread cubes and fry for a few minutes on each side, or until
golden brown all over. Now drizzle over the Sabzi Sauce and toss the cubes
until they are coated but retain some crunch. Remove the pan from the heat
and set aside.

Transfer the roasted tomatoes, chillies and garlic cloves (pop them out of
their skins first) to a food processor or a blender and blitz until smooth, then
pour the mixture into a saucepan and add the boiling water, vinegar, sugar
and a generous amount of salt. Bring the mixture to a gentle simmer. Once
hot, taste and adjust the seasoning as required, then serve immediately, with
the croutons on top and an extra drizzle of olive oil, if desired.

PIES, BREADS & PASTRIES

BUTTERNUT, FETA & CHILLI ROLLS

I first came up with this recipe for the launch of my second cookbook, Sirocco. I wanted something delicious and substantial for those who didn't eat meat as well as those who did. This recipe went on to become a favourite at pop-up feasts in all sorts of different shapes and sizes. If butternut squash isn't your thing, it also works beautifully with other types of squash when in season.

1kg butternut squash (unpeeled), halved and deseeded

olive oil

2 teaspoons chilli flakes

1 teaspoon ground cinnamon

1 fat garlic clove, crushed

200g feta cheese, crumbled

1 small packet (about 30g) of flat leaf parsley, finely chopped

1 x 320g ready-rolled all-butter puff pastry sheet

1 egg, beaten

1 teaspoon nigella seeds

Maldon sea salt flakes and freshly ground black pepper

MAKES 8

Preheat the oven to 210°C (190°C fan), Gas Mark 6½.

Place the squash halves, with their cut sides facing up, in a baking tray and drizzle over a little olive oil. Roast for about 50 minutes, or until the flesh is cooked through and soft. (Don't switch off the oven.)

When cool enough to handle, use a spoon to scoop the butternut squash flesh out of the skins and into a mixing bowl. Add the chilli, cinnamon and garlic, season with a generous amount of salt and pepper, then mash it all together. Now gently fold in the feta and parsley. Set aside.

Increase the oven temperature to 220°C (200°C fan), Gas Mark 7. Line a baking tray with baking paper.

Cut the pastry into 8 squares. Divide the filling into 8 portions. Shape one portion of filling into a sausage shape and place it diagonally across one of the pastry squares. Fold the pastry corners over the filling, pinching together – the filling will remain exposed at each end. Repeat with the remaining pastry and filling. Transfer the parcels to the prepared tray, brush with the beaten egg, scatter over the nigella seeds and bake for about 25 minutes, or until deep golden brown. Serve hot or at room temperature according to your preference.

POTATO, SPRING ONION & GOATS' CHEESE HAND PIES

I think that what the British don't know about savoury pie making simply isn't worth knowing, and I don't just mean meat pies. Some of the best, most comforting pies are meat-free, such as the classic homity pie, filled with nothing more than potato, cheese, leek and onion – quite possibly one of my favourite pies of all time. This recipe combines similar ingredients in a simple puff pastry crust – perfect for summer bites and winter nights.

250g waxy potatoes (such as Charlotte or new potatoes)

250g soft goats' cheese

1 tablespoon dried wild oregano

3 fat spring onions, thinly sliced from root to tip

½ small packet (about 15g) of tarragon, leaves finely chopped

1 x 320g ready-rolled all-butter puff pastry sheet

1 egg, beaten

1 teaspoon nigella seeds

Maldon sea salt flakes and freshly ground black pepper

MAKES 6

Boil the potatoes for 15 minutes, then drain and leave to cool.

Halve the cooled potatoes lengthways down the centre, then slice each potato half into half moons.

Put the goats' cheese, oregano, spring onions and a good amount of salt and pepper into a large mixing bowl and mash the ingredients together, then add the potato pieces and tarragon. Mix well until all the ingredients are evenly combined.

Preheat the oven to 200°C (180°C fan), Gas Mark 6. Line a large baking tray with baking paper.

Cut the pastry into 6 squares. Divide the filling into 6 portions and shape each portion into balls. Place a ball of filling in the centre of each pastry square, then gather up the pastry corners and pinch together to seal (it doesn't need to be perfect). Transfer the parcels to the prepared baking tray, brush with the beaten egg, scatter over the nigella seeds and bake for 25–30 minutes, or until golden brown. Serve immediately.

ROAST VEGETABLE BASTILLA

Bastilla is traditionally a celebratory Moroccan dish made with pigeon, but I've made this with leftover roasted vegetables – which is how this version was born. You can pretty much throw anything together with Moroccan spices, dried fruits and nuts and turn it into something beautiful, so this makes an impressive centrepiece – yet ridiculously easy to make.

1 teaspoon cayenne pepper

2 teaspoons ground cinnamon

2 teaspoons turmeric

2 teaspoons ground cumin

2 teaspoons garlic granules

750g celeriac, peeled and cut into 2.5cm cubes

750g butternut squash, peeled, deseeded and cut into 2.5cm cubes

500g carrots, peeled and cut into 2.5cm chunks

500g parsnips, peeled and cut into 2.5cm chunks

olive oil

50g flaked almonds

50g pine nuts

100g ready-to-eat dried apricots, roughly chopped

50g flat leaf parsley, finely chopped

4 tablespoons clear honey

finely grated zest and juice of 1 unwaxed lemon

6 sheets of filo pastry (each about 48 x 25cm)

75g butter, melted

1 egg, beaten

Maldon sea salt flakes and freshly ground black pepper

SERVES 6–8

Preheat the oven to 220°C (200°C fan), Gas Mark 7. Line your 2 largest baking trays with baking paper.

Mix all the spices and garlic granules together in a bowl. Put the vegetables into a large mixing bowl. Sprinkle over the spice blend, drizzle liberally with olive oil and season generously with salt and pepper, then use your hands to mix until the vegetables are well coated. Divide the mixture between the 2 prepared trays and roast for about 45 minutes, opening the oven door halfway through the cooking time to allow the steam to escape. Once the edges of the vegetables start to brown, remove the trays from the oven and allow the vegetables to cool. At this point you can refrigerate the vegetables to use later.

Roughly chop the cooled root vegetables and put them into a large mixing bowl along with the nuts, dried apricots, parsley, honey and lemon zest and juice. Add a generous extra seasoning of salt and mix well using a large spoon, ensuring you don't mash the vegetables too much (but mashing them a little is actually quite nice!)

Preheat the oven to 220°C (200°C fan), Gas Mark 7. Line the largest baking tray you have with baking paper.

Select a large frying pan, about 26cm in diameter. Line the pan with a pastry sheet, leaving the end overhanging (you need plenty of overhang to be able to fold this over the top of the filling), then lay the remaining pastry sheets on top in a clockwise direction. Tip the filling mixture into the centre and flatten it out to make a firm disc. Fold the overhanging pastry over the filling and brush the pastry with the melted butter to seal the pastry together.

Place the prepared baking tray upside-down over the pan and invert the bastilla on to the tray. Brush the top of the pastry with the beaten egg. Bake for 25–30 minutes, or until golden brown. Serve immediately.

CARAMELIZED ONION, FETA & OLIVE TART

Savoury tarts are so versatile – you can bake one for dinner, then serve up leftovers with a salad for lunch the next day. It's lovely for breakfast or brunch, too, and it makes a fantastic addition as part of a bigger feast. Tarts are easy to make. I sometimes cheat and use shop-bought pastry if I'm short of time (use a 500g block of ready-made shortcrust pastry, then roll it out and bake following the method below). If you're making the pastry, prepare a double batch of dough and freeze half – it'll make life so much easier when you next make a tart.

225g plain flour, plus extra for dusting
100g cold salted butter, cut into
    small cubes
3–4 tablespoons cold water

For the filling
vegetable oil
2 large onions, halved and thinly sliced
    into half moons
1 teaspoon wild thyme leaves
250g ricotta cheese
200g feta cheese, finely crumbled
1 large egg
1 teaspoon pul biber chilli flakes
1 teaspoon garlic granules
16 pitted Kalamata olives, plus a few
    extra to garnish
pinch of Maldon sea salt flakes
freshly ground black pepper

SERVES 8–10

First make the pastry. Put the flour into a large mixing bowl, then rub in the butter with your fingertips until the mixture resembles fine breadcrumbs. Add the cold water and mix to a stiff dough. Roll the dough into a ball, wrap it in clingfilm and refrigerate for at least 30 minutes.

To make the filling, drizzle a little vegetable oil into a large frying pan set over a medium-low heat. Add the onion and thyme and cook slowly, stirring regularly, until the onion has caramelized and is golden in colour – do not allow it to crisp up or burn. Once cooked, set aside to cool.

Select a 24cm-diameter tart tin. Tear a large square of clingfilm and place it on your work surface. Dust generously with flour, then set the pastry dough on top, dust that with flour and cover it loosely with another layer of clingfilm. Using a rolling pin, roll out the dough until it is slightly larger than your tin (it should be nice and thin). Remove the top layer of clingfilm and carefully transfer the dough into the tin – don't worry if it breaks, as you can easily patch it up later with dough trimmings. Push the dough gently into the edges of the tin, leaving a little overhanging. Now sweep the rolling pin across the top of the tin to cut off the overhanging dough. Use the trimmings to patch up any cracks or holes. Cover with clingfilm and refrigerate for at least 20 minutes.

Preheat the oven to 200°C (180°C fan), Gas Mark 6.

In a mixing bowl, combine the ricotta, feta and egg until the mixture is smooth. Add the pul biber, garlic granules, olives and caramelized onions, and season with the salt and a generous amount of black pepper. Combine well.

Pour the filling into the pastry case and garnish with a few extra olives, if desired. Bake for 30–35 minutes, or until cooked through and brown on top. Allow to cool slightly before serving.

DATE-STUFFED NAAN

Many years ago I worked at a Michelin-starred Indian restaurant, and the one thing I've never forgotten is their mind-blowing date naan. Sadly, I never learnt how to make it, but the memory of its chocolate-like filling against chewy, charred bread has stayed with me and inspired this date bread. Although my version is not fired in a Tandoor clay oven, it is still every bit as satisfying.

350g strong bread flour, plus extra
    for dusting

7g sachet fast-action dried yeast

good pinch of Maldon sea salt flakes

150g Greek yogurt

125ml lukewarm water, plus extra
    if needed

2 tablespoons olive oil

1 tablespoon sesame seeds

20g unsalted butter, melted

For the filling

300g best-quality dates, stoned and
    roughly chopped

50g unsalted butter

2 tablespoons clear honey

1 tablespoon ground cinnamon

SERVES 6-8

Mix the flour, yeast and salt together in a large mixing bowl, then add the yogurt, measured lukewarm water and olive oil and use your hands to combine the mixture in a dough – add a little extra flour or water, if needed, to bring the dough together. Knead the dough in the bowl for 1 minute, then allow to rest for 10 minutes. Knead the dough again for 1 minute, then cover the bowl with a clean tea towel and leave somewhere warm for 1½ hours to rise.

Put the filling ingredients into a small saucepan over a medium-low heat and cook for a few minutes, until heated through. Take the pan off the heat and mash the mixture to a paste. This should happen fairly easily, as the dates will break down quickly. Set aside.

Preheat the oven to 220°C (200°C fan), Gas Mark 7. Line your largest baking tray with baking paper.

Once the dough has risen, knock it back and divide it into 2 equal balls. Lightly dust your work surface with flour and roll out each ball of dough to a thickness of just under 5mm, in any shape you like – circular or irregular – but just ensure they are both roughly the same shape.

Lay one sheet of dough on the prepared tray. Spread the date paste across it, allowing a border of 2.5cm. Place the other sheet of dough on top and tuck the edges under the first sheet of dough, then pinch the edges together to seal the parcel as best you can. Lastly, scatter over the sesame seeds and press them into the dough (a rolling pin helps with this). Now brush the dough all over with the melted butter, ensuring you brush right to the edges. Bake for 18–20 minutes, or until the naan is cooked through and nicely browned on top. Allow to cool before serving.

PERSIAN SWEET SAFFRON BREADS

Sheermal is a sweet, saffron-tinted Persian bread and a treasured memory from my childhood in London when the local Persian restaurants sold them – they're now impossible to find. This is my own lighter version – no kneading is required – and I would encourage you to eat it with spicy dishes such as curries, soups and stews, although a bit of feta and a drizzle of honey would also do nicely.

1g (about a pinch) saffron threads, ground to a powder using a pestle and mortar

3 tablespoons boiling water

300g strong bread flour, plus extra for dusting

3.5g (½ sachet) fast-action dried yeast

good pinch of Maldon sea salt flakes

50g caster sugar

60g butter, melted

150ml milk, plus extra for glazing

1 teaspoon black or white sesame seeds

MAKES 4

Put the saffron powder into a small cup and pour over the boiling water. Leave to steep until the liquid is cool.

Put the flour, yeast, salt and sugar into a large mixing bowl and mix well. Add the melted butter, milk and the cooled saffron solution and mix well to form a dough. Roll the dough into a smooth ball and place it in a bowl. Cover the bowl with clingfilm, then cover with a clean tea towel and leave somewhere warm for 1½ hours to rise.

Preheat the oven to 200°C (180°C fan), Gas Mark 6. Line a large baking sheet with baking paper.

Once the dough has risen, knock it back and divide it into 4 equal portions. Lightly dust your work surface with flour and roll out each portion of dough into a round roughly 1cm thick. Transfer the dough rounds to the prepared baking sheet. Brush the surfaces with milk, then sprinkle one-quarter of the sesame seeds over each round. Bake for 12–15 minutes, or until brown around the edges. Transfer to a wire rack to cool, then serve warm.

ZA'ATAR-RUBBED PITTAS

This is my take on a popular Lebanese flatbread snack called maneesh. If I'm honest, I have a pitta addiction, and rubbing the top of pitta bread with za'atar and olive oil is absolutely delicious. Za'atar wasn't something I used much until I became a chef, and I never fully understood its potential until I started using it at home. This versatile herb blend can be used with bread, salads, cheese, in marinades and rubs and so much more.

For the za'atar blend
10g dried wild thyme
10g dried wild oregano
10g dried marjoram
2 tablespoons sumac
2 tablespoons sesame seeds,
    lightly toasted
1 tablespoon Maldon sea salt flakes

MAKES 1 JAR

3 tablespoons olive oil, for the za'atar oil

For the pittas
5g fast-action dried yeast
150ml lukewarm water
250g plain flour, plus extra for dusting
1 teaspoon fine sea salt
2 tablespoons olive oil

MAKES 6

To make the za'atar blend, use a spice or coffee grinder to grind the thyme, oregano and marjoram together just until they break down (you can also use a pestle and mortar, but it won't work as well). Decant the mixture into a bowl, stir in the sumac, sesame seeds and salt, then pour into an airtight container. It will last for up to a year if stored in a dark, cool, dry place.

To make a za'atar oil, combine 4 teaspoons of the za'atar blend with the olive oil. Stir well and set aside.

To make the pittas, dissolve the yeast in the lukewarm water and leave the mixture to sit for 5 minutes. Put the flour, salt, olive oil and yeast mixture into a mixing bowl and mix together with your hands to form a dough. Knead the dough in the bowl for a few minutes, then cover the bowl with clingfilm and leave it somewhere warm for 1 hour to rise.

Divide the dough into 6 equal balls. Lightly dust your work surface with flour and roll out each ball of dough into a round about 5mm thick. Leave to rest for 10 minutes.

When you are ready to cook the pittas, heat a large, heavy-based frying pan over a medium-high heat. Place a dough round into the hot frying pan (without any oil) and cook for about 45 seconds on one side, or until the edges begin to come away from the pan, then flip it over and cook for a further 30–45 seconds, or until very lightly browned. Keep the pitta warm while you cook the remaining dough rounds in the same way.

Divide the za'atar oil equally between the 6 hot pittas and rub it into the surface. Serve immediately.

SALADS FOR
ALL SEASONS

BLACKBERRY, BEETROOT & ZA'ATAR GOATS' CHEESE SALAD

Nothing reminds me more of England than all the gorgeous berries and autumnal fruit that we produce in abundance. I like to combine Middle Eastern ingredients with Western produce if the flavours work, and this combination does exactly that – sweet but tart blackberries with creamy soft goats' cheese balls dusted in my beloved herb mix, za'atar. This is now one of my favourite autumnal salads, and once you try it, you'll see why.

200g soft goats' cheese

2–3 tablespoons Za'atar Blend
  (*see* page 86)

150g mixed salad leaves

300g cooked beetroot (not in vinegar),
  quartered

250g blackberries (reserve 6 for the
  dressing)

freshly ground black pepper

For the dressing

6 blackberries (reserved from the salad
  ingredients)

1 tablespoon red wine vinegar

2 tablespoons olive oil

pinch of Maldon sea salt flakes

SERVES 4–6

First make the dressing. In a small bowl or using a pestle and mortar, bash 6 of the blackberries until puréed, then add the vinegar, olive oil and salt and mix well. Set aside.

To prepare the salad, divide the goats' cheese into 12 equal-sized cubes and roll them into smooth balls. Lightly dust with the za'atar blend and roll in your palms to ensure the za'atar sticks to the surface. Set the balls on a plate and refrigerate until needed.

When you're ready to serve, select a large, wide board or platter and spread the salad leaves across it. Arrange the beetroot quarters and the blackberries around the board or plate, then season with pepper and drizzle over the dressing. Lastly, dot with the goats' cheese balls and serve immediately.

MILLI'S CHARRED SWEETCORN SALAD

Once in a blue moon, I sheepishly agree to cook a meal for a talented chef friend of mine named Milli Taylor. Milli is one of those doubly talented individuals who not only makes food that tastes amazing, but her creations look beautiful, too. She always enjoys my salads, and this one in particular – a rainbow salad, as she calls it. She has good taste – it's also a favourite of mine.

2 sweetcorn cobs

400g can hearts of palm, drained and cut diagonally into 1cm-thick slices

300g baby tomatoes, halved

½ red onion, sliced into half moons

½ small packet (about 15g) of fresh coriander, roughly chopped

For the dressing

3 tablespoons Greek yogurt

1 tablespoon harissa

juice of ½ fat lime

Maldon sea salt flakes and freshly ground black pepper

SERVES 4–6

Mix the dressing ingredients together in a small bowl and season to taste with salt and pepper. Set aside.

Cook the corn cobs in a saucepan of simmering water for 10 minutes, or until soft but not completely tender, then drain. Preheat a griddle pan over a high heat and griddle the corn cobs for 5 minutes, turning occasionally, until charred in places. Remove from the heat and transfer to a chopping board. Hold the sweetcorn cobs vertically and, using a sharp knife, cut down to slice off the kernels, then put them in a mixing bowl.

Arrange the hearts of palm, corn kernels, tomato and red onion on a serving platter. Dot with the dressing, then scatter over the coriander and serve.

CRUNCHY TOFU SALAD

WITH TAMARIND & MISO DRESSING

I am a recent convert to tofu and have concluded that it is an excellent carrier of flavour, and when combined with some carefully selected punchy ingredients – in this instance a lovely crisp and crunchy salad base – it is absolutely perfect.

200g white cabbage, finely shredded

200g red cabbage, finely shredded

1 small red pepper, cored, deseeded and cut into thin strips

1 small yellow pepper, cored, deseeded and cut into thin strips

3 celery sticks, very thinly sliced

4 spring onions, thinly sliced diagonally from root to tip

100g salted roasted peanuts

1 small packet (about 30g) of fresh coriander, roughly chopped

400g firm tofu, cut into 2.5cm cubes

For the dressing

3 tablespoons unsweetened tamarind paste

3 tablespoons white miso paste

3 tablespoons clear honey

3 tablespoons olive oil

1 teaspoon cayenne pepper

1 teaspoon ground cinnamon

finely grated zest and juice of ½ unwaxed lemon

Maldon sea salt flakes and freshly ground black pepper

SERVES 4

Preheat a nonstick griddle pan over a high heat.

Meanwhile, combine all the salad ingredients, except the tofu, in a large mixing bowl.

Mix the dressing ingredients together in a small jug and season well with salt and pepper.

Place the tofu cubes in a shallow bowl and dress them with roughly one-third of the dressing. Pour the remainder of the dressing over the salad and toss the salad with your hands to ensure the ingredients are well coated.

Chargrill the tofu pieces for about 1 minute on each side, or until dark char marks appear.

Transfer the salad to a large, wide bowl, dot with the grilled tofu and serve.

ORANGE, OLIVE & ONION SALAD

I am one of those weirdos who is obsessed with transforming vegetables into sweet dishes and adding fruit into savoury salads. The truth is, nothing beats a refreshing, juicy burst of fruit to complement the kind of food that I make. More importantly, the gentle sweetness and acidity cut through spice and chilli heat perfectly. This particular salad is a great favourite of mine, as I am forever zesting oranges for all sorts of recipes and often left with the whole fruit – this is the perfect way to use them up.

4 oranges (blood oranges are a great
    choice, when in season)
½ red onion, very thinly sliced into
    half moons
2 handfuls of green olives, pitted
few sprigs of mint, leaves picked,
    rolled up tightly and thinly sliced
    into ribbons
good handful of pine nuts
2 pinches of pul biber chilli flakes
extra virgin olive oil, for drizzling
Maldon sea salt flakes and freshly
    ground black pepper

SERVES 4–6

You'll need a sharp knife to peel the oranges. With each fruit, cut a disc of peel off the top and base of the orange. Then, working from the top of the fruit downwards, cut away the remaining peel and pith in strips until the entire orange is peeled. Slice the orange widthways into 4 or 5 slices.

Arrange the orange slices on a large platter or board. Season well with salt and pepper, then scatter over the onion slivers, followed by the olives, fresh mint and pine nuts. Sprinkle over the pul biber. Drizzle over a little olive oil and serve immediately.

ROOT RIBBON SALAD
WITH POMEGRANATE

*I've always said that if I have to eat a salad, it better have a lot going for it flavour-wise.
I've also realized that the crunchier you make a salad, the more you chew, and the quicker you feel full.
I do wish the same rule applied to eating pies and heavier food, but that's life, eh? This wonderfully
sweet-tasting salad is packed full of flavour, crunch and visual appeal. Hard to beat, really.*

½ small white cabbage, finely shredded

150g dried cranberries

1 bunch of spring onions, finely sliced
    diagonally from root to tip

150g toasted cashew nuts

2 large parsnips, peeled and cut into
    ribbons with a vegetable peeler

2 large carrots, peeled and cut into
    ribbons with a vegetable peeler

½ small celeriac, peeled and cut into
    ribbons with a vegetable peeler

30g dill, finely chopped

30g mint, leaves picked, rolled up
    tightly and thinly sliced into ribbons

200g pomegranate seeds

For the dressing

1 heaped teaspoon cumin seeds, toasted
    and roughly crushed using
    a pestle and mortar

1 heaped teaspoon coriander seeds,
    toasted and roughly crushed using
    a pestle and mortar

1 heaped tablespoon rose harissa

3 tablespoons rice wine vinegar

2–3 tablespoons clear honey

good drizzle of extra virgin olive oil

Maldon sea salt flakes and freshly
    ground black pepper

SERVES 6–8

Mix the dressing ingredients together in a small bowl and season to taste with salt and pepper.

Put the cabbage, cranberries, spring onion, cashews and the dressing into a large mixing bowl and mix well with your hands. Add the parsnip, carrot and celeriac ribbons and mix again. Now add the herbs and pomegranate seeds and toss through. Check the seasoning and adjust if necessary, then toss one last time and serve immediately.

SPICED BUTTERMILK SALAD

*The first time I saw a Caesar salad served with quartered heads of lettuce, I was horrified! Since then,
I have come to embrace the 'lazy lettuce method', as I now call it. While this isn't a classic Caesar
(it pains me to eat a salad with more calories and fat than a burger), it is a lovely variation,
and the eggs make it a complete and rather filling meal.*

4 eggs

2 pitta breads

2 large Romaine (Cos) lettuce,
    quartered lengthways

1 long shallot, thinly sliced

4 radishes, thinly sliced

1 heaped teaspoon sumac

For the spiced buttermilk dressing

300ml buttermilk

1 teaspoon ground coriander

1 teaspoon garlic granules

½ teaspoon celery salt

1 generous tablespoon olive oil

freshly ground black pepper

SERVES 4

First make the buttermilk dressing. Mix the buttermilk, coriander, garlic granules, celery salt and olive oil in a jug and season with some black pepper. Set aside.

Pour boiling water from a kettle into a saucepan and set over a medium-high heat. Once the water is bubbling, carefully lower in the eggs and boil for 6 minutes. Drain the eggs, then place them under cold running water to arrest the cooking process. When they are cool enough to handle, peel, then halve each egg.

Toast the pitta breads in a toaster until they have dried out, then cut into small cubes. (Alternatively, cut the pitta into cubes, place on a baking tray and bake in a preheated oven at 180°C (160°C fan), Gas Mark 4 for 12 minutes.)

Arrange the lettuce quarters in a large serving dish. Arrange the egg halves in the bowl, followed by the shallot and radish. Drizzle over the dressing, sprinkle over the sumac for a final flourish, then serve.

BLOOD ORANGE, PECAN & CANNELLINI SALAD

WITH SAUTÉED FENNEL

Vibrant, refreshing, satisfying and delicious: all the things I want from a salad. This one is perfect served as a main meal or a side dish. Being a colourful creation, it makes a great centrepiece at any time of year, whether you use blood oranges or not.

olive oil

2 large fennel bulbs, quartered, then cut into rough 5mm-thick slices

4 best-quality blood oranges (or use regular oranges)

100g mixed salad leaves (Continental or Italian mix; rocket and watercress work especially well)

400g can cannellini beans, drained and rinsed

100g pecan nuts

75g golden raisins

1 small packet (about 10g) of chives, each stem cut into thirds

Maldon sea salt flakes and freshly ground black pepper

For the dressing

2 tablespoons red wine vinegar

1 tablespoon clear honey

1 teaspoon ground cinnamon

½ teaspoon cayenne pepper (optional)

1 tablespoon water

generous drizzle of extra virgin olive oil

Maldon sea salt flakes and freshly ground black pepper

SERVES 4–6

Set a large frying pan over a medium heat and drizzle in a little olive oil. Add the fennel slices and sauté for a few minutes, until slightly softened and the edges turn golden brown. Transfer to a bowl using a slotted spoon, season with a little salt and pepper and set aside.

You'll need a sharp knife to peel the oranges. With each fruit, cut a disc of peel off the top and base of the orange. Then, working from the top of the fruit downwards, cut away the remaining peel and pith in strips until the entire orange is peeled. Slice the orange widthways into 1cm-thick slices.

Arrange the mixed leaves on a large platter or in a shallow salad bowl. Scatter over the cannellini beans and arrange the orange and pecans across the platter. Add the fennel, then scatter over the raisins and chives.

Mix the dressing ingredients together in a small jug, then drizzle the dressing over the salad. Serve immediately.

ROASTED PEPPERS & POMEGRANATE VINAIGRETTE

I love roasting peppers. Since I have never had a gas hob in my kitchen, or an outdoor space to barbecue at home (yes, I know – shock horror!), I roast them in the oven. It's easy, and I think they are just as good as chargrilled ones. A subtle element of vinegar complements their intense sweetness, and, with the added crunch and earthy flavour of pistachio, this dish is one of the most simple yet intensely flavoured salads there is.

500g small or baby mixed peppers or
    6 long pointed red or yellow peppers,
    halved, cored and deseeded
3 tablespoons olive oil
50g pistachio nuts, roughly chopped
Maldon sea salt flakes

For the dressing
3 tablespoons pomegranate molasses
2 tablespoons red wine vinegar
2 tablespoons olive oil
Maldon sea salt flakes

SERVES 6

Preheat your oven to its highest temperature setting. Line a baking tray with baking paper.

Place the peppers on the prepared baking tray with their skin sides facing up. Drizzle over the olive oil, season well with salt and roast for 14–16 minutes, or until nicely charred.

Mix the ingredients for the dressing together in a small bowl and season with a little salt to taste.

Arrange the peppers on a platter and spoon over the dressing. Scatter over the pistachios and serve.

CABBAGE & SESAME SALAD

White cabbage is hugely underrated. Although it is most commonly used in coleslaw, it has so much more potential. It is the Japanese use of simple shredded cabbage on the side of katsu (all things breadcrumbed and fried) that inspired this salad, which has a great depth of flavour and is very moreish.

600–650g white cabbage,
   finely shredded
1 tablespoon nigella seeds
50g toasted sesame seeds
2 teaspoons pul biber chilli flakes

For the dressing
1 tablespoon sesame oil
3 tablespoons rice vinegar
2 heaped tablespoons tahini
1 tablespoon clear honey
Maldon sea salt flakes and freshly
   ground black pepper

SERVES 6–8

Put the shredded cabbage into a large mixing bowl.

To make the dressing, mix the sesame oil, vinegar and tahini together in a jug, using a light touch because tahini stiffens if you over-mix it. Stir in the honey and season with a generous amount of salt and pepper.

Pour the dressing over the cabbage and mix well. Add the nigella and sesame seeds and pul biber, mix again, then serve immediately.

COURGETTE, PEA & SPINACH SALAD

WITH PRESERVED LEMON DRESSING

This is one of those salads that is so green and vibrant that you just know you are being healthy eating it, but moreover, it has a wonderful flavour and texture – the sharp spike of preserved lemons gives it the perfect tang and the crunchy pumpkin seeds finish it off – it's the perfect summer salad. I sometimes eat this stirred through cold cooked pasta with a little extra feta and some olive oil for a more filling meal.

150g fresh peas

50g pumpkin seeds

2 courgettes, coarsely grated

150g baby spinach leaves

For the dressing

2 teaspoons coriander seeds

4 preserved lemons

4 tablespoons olive oil

freshly ground black pepper

SERVES 4–6

Bring a small saucepan of water to the boil, add the peas and blanch for 2 minutes. Drain the peas and rinse them in cold water, then drain well and set aside.

Toast the coriander seeds for the dressing in a dry frying pan over a medium heat for about 1 minute, until they release their aroma. Remove from the heat, transfer to a pestle and mortar and crush them lightly, grinding just enough to crack the seeds.

In the same frying pan, toast the pumpkin seeds for 3–4 minutes, or until they are slightly charred around the edges and have some colour. Transfer to a bowl and set aside to cool.

To make the dressing, you can either chop the preserved lemons very finely and purée them by hand using a pestle and mortar, or blitz them in a mini blender. Transfer them to a bowl, season with black pepper, stir in the olive oil, then the crushed coriander seeds and mix well (you won't need salt, as the preserved lemons are already salty).

Put the grated courgette, spinach leaves and the peas into a large mixing bowl, pour over the dressing and toss very lightly using your hands to coat the leaves. Arrange the dressed leaves on a large platter and scatter with the roasted pumpkin seeds. Serve immediately.

RED & WHITE RICE SALAD
WITH BUTTERNUT SQUASH & POMEGRANATE

This is what my family knows as my Thanksgiving salad. Despite being British, many of my family are based in the US and we need no excuse to gather en masse at any time of the year. This salad is my annual contribution to the festivities. I always make a ridiculous amount of it so that it can be given away to various people as takeaway.

1–1.2kg butternut squash, peeled, deseeded and cut into 2.5cm cubes

olive oil

3 tablespoons cumin seeds

150g basmati rice

150g red Camargue rice

200g dried cranberries

100g toasted flaked almonds

100g flat leaf parsley, finely chopped

1 large red onion, very finely diced

finely grated zest and juice of 1 large unwaxed orange

2 teaspoons ground cinnamon

4–5 tablespoons red wine vinegar

4 heaped tablespoons clear honey

300g pomegranate seeds

Maldon sea salt flakes and freshly ground black pepper

SERVES 6–8

Preheat the oven to 220°C (200°C fan), Gas Mark 7. Line a baking tray with baking paper.

Place the butternut squash pieces on the prepared baking tray and drizzle generously with olive oil. Scatter over the cumin seeds and season generously with salt and pepper. Mix using your hands to ensure each cube is evenly coated in the oil and seasoning. Roast for 40–45 minutes, or until the edges of the squash are browned and charred. Once cooked, set aside to cool.

Bring 2 saucepans of water to the boil and cook the 2 different varieties of rice according to the packet instructions. Drain and rinse thoroughly under cold running water until completely cool, then drain well.

Put the cranberries, almonds, parsley, onion and rice into a large mixing bowl and mix well. Add the orange zest and juice, cinnamon, 5 tablespoons of olive oil, the vinegar, honey and a generous amount of salt and pepper and stir well. Gently incorporate the cubes of cooled butternut squash into the salad along with the pomegranate seeds. Arrange the salad in a large bowl and serve at room temperature.

MOGHRABIEH SALAD

Despite its exotic name, moghrabieh is essentially giant couscous, or small dots of pasta. Infinitely versatile, it works very well in stews, soups, salads and on its own as a main dish, like you might serve a pilaf. This lovely salad is great at any time of year – perfect for warmer weather, but with gentle spicing and comfort for the colder months, too. If you can find golden raisins, they are well worth it – I've used them to convert many a raisin-hater and they give a wonderful burst of sweetness with every bite. This salad is even better the next day, so make it the day before and refrigerate to allow the spices to intensify.

300g moghrabieh (giant couscous)

2 tablespoons olive oil

1 large red pepper, cored, deseeded and
    cut into 1cm dice

1 large yellow pepper, cored, deseeded
    and cut into 1cm dice

100g pine nuts

2 small packets (about 60g) of dill,
    finely chopped

100g flat leaf parsley, roughly chopped

Maldon sea salt flakes and freshly
    ground black pepper

For the dressing

3 tablespoons olive oil

3 tablespoons red wine vinegar

3 tablespoons clear honey

2 teaspoons ground cinnamon

1 teaspoon chilli flakes

SERVES 6–8

Boil the moghrabieh according to the packet instructions. Drain the grains and rinse them thoroughly under cold running water until completely cool, then drain well. Set aside.

Heat the olive oil in a saucepan over a medium-high heat. Add the peppers and sauté for about 8 minutes, or until soft and browned at the edges. Set aside to cool.

Heat a small frying pan over a medium heat, add the pine nuts and toast for a few minutes, shaking the pan until golden all over, then remove from the heat and set aside.

Mix the dressing ingredients together in a small bowl and set aside.

Put the cooked moghrabieh into a large bowl. Add the peppers, herbs and pine nuts and mix well until they are evenly distributed. Season generously with salt and pepper. Now pour over the dressing and combine. Leave to rest for at least 30 minutes to allow the flavours to develop before serving.

SMOKED AUBERGINE, PEPPER & WALNUT SALAD
WITH POMEGRANATE

I always associate smoked aubergine with the East. Most Middle Eastern nations seem to have a version of them, and the roots of many of these recipes relate to the world's most simple and primitive cooking technique – food plus fire, which as we all know equals nothing short of magic. From meat to every kind of vegetable and even some fruits, very few edibles aren't somehow improved by the kiss of fire, and aubergine is definitely my favourite.

4 large aubergines

3 large red peppers

50g chopped walnuts

1 small packet (about 30g) of flat leaf parsley, roughly chopped (reserve some for garnish)

2 fat garlic cloves, crushed

6 tablespoons olive oil, plus extra to serve

juice of ½ lemon

pinch of ground cinnamon

75ml pomegranate molasses

100g pomegranate seeds

Maldon sea salt flakes and freshly ground black pepper

flatbread, to serve (*see* page 38)

SERVES 6–8

Blister and char the aubergines and peppers, either on a barbecue, flame grill or on the flame of your gas hob. Really blacken the skins until they are hardened and completely burnt. (Lining your hob with kitchen foil will prevent you having to deal with a very heavy clean-up, as the juices can be messy.)

Place the aubergines on a heatproof surface or tray and leave to cool for about 20 minutes, until they are just warm and you are able to handle them.

Place the peppers in a food bag, tie it closed and set aside to allow them to sweat for about 20 minutes. Once this time has elapsed, the blackened, charred skins should slide easily off the peppers until you are left with just the roasted flesh. Roughly chop the flesh and place in a large mixing bowl.

Using a large metal spoon, scoop out the flesh of the aubergines and place it in a fine-mesh sieve to drain off any of the excess juices. Discard the charred skins. Roughly chop the flesh into smallish chunks and add them to the roasted peppers. Mix together gently.

Add the walnuts, parsley, garlic, olive oil, lemon juice, cinnamon and salt and pepper to the bowl, and give all the ingredients a good mix until they are evenly combined.

Serve the aubergine smoothed out flat on a large platter. Drizzle with the pomegranate molasses, scatter over the reserved parsley and the pomegranate seeds, then add a light drizzle of olive oil. Serve immediately with flatbreads.

MOREISH MAINS

SMOKY BLACK-EYED BEAN & TOMATO STEW

Simplicity is best. That's what I had in mind when I came up with the recipe for this stew, where the whole is greater than the sum of its parts. It provides the most perfect, comforting bowl of warmth that is welcome as a lunch or dinner, and any leftovers on toast topped with an egg make a great breakfast. A little cheese on top works wonders, but I really like it just as it comes, perhaps with a hunk of crusty bread on the side.

olive oil

2 onions, finely chopped

4 fat garlic cloves, thinly sliced

1 teaspoon chilli flakes

1 teaspoon ground cinnamon

1 teaspoon smoked paprika

2 teaspoons ground cumin

2 teaspoons cocoa powder

2 x 400g cans chopped tomatoes
   (reserve the liquid from 1 can,
   drain the second can)

2 x 400g cans black-eyed beans,
   drained and rinsed

Maldon sea salt flakes and freshly
   ground black pepper

SERVES 4–6

Add enough olive oil to coat the base of a large saucepan and set over a medium heat. Add the onion and cook for 6–8 minutes, or until softened and translucent. Stir in the garlic and cook for a few more minutes until softened.

Add all the spices, the cocoa powder and a generous amount of salt and pepper to the saucepan and stir well. Now mix in the tomatoes, then reduce the heat to a gentle simmer, cover the pan with a lid and cook slowly for a further 30 minutes, or until the tomato has thickened and cooked down to a sauce.

Taste the stew and adjust the seasoning if necessary, then stir in the beans. If the stew is too thick, use a little of the reserved canning liquid from the tomatoes to loosen the sauce. Cook for 15–20 minutes to warm the beans through and allow them to take on the flavours of the spices, then serve.

CHICKPEA, PANEER, SPINACH, & PRESERVED LEMON STEW

This full-flavoured stew is delicious and the preserved lemons give it a lovely citrus zing. A little bread or rice on the side is all you need to provide the perfect vehicle for the soft morsels of paneer.

vegetable oil

2 onions, halved and sliced into
   half moons

1 heaped teaspoon turmeric

2 tablespoons dried mint

1 large garlic bulb, cloves peeled

500g baby spinach leaves

400g can chickpeas

250ml boiling water

6–8 preserved lemons, halved

225g paneer, cut into 12 cubes

Maldon sea salt flakes and freshly
   ground black pepper

SERVES 4-6

Put a drizzle of vegetable oil into a large saucepan set over a medium heat. Add the onion and cook for 6–8 minutes, or until softened. Stir in the turmeric and mint and cook for 1 minute, then mix in the garlic cloves. Cook for a few minutes until the garlic has softened a little, then stir in the spinach. Cover the pan with a lid and cook for 2–3 minutes, or until the spinach has wilted.

Season the mixture in the saucepan generously with salt and pepper, then add the chickpeas and stir in the boiling water. Reduce the heat to low, part-cover the pan with the lid and simmer for 20 minutes, until it has thickened to a broth and is not too watery.

Check the seasoning and adjust it if necessary, then mix the preserved lemon halves into the saucepan. Now stir in the paneer. Cook for a further 15 minutes, then serve immediately with bread or rice.

HARISSA PASTA DOUGH

In case you need more proof of the versatility of harissa, this fresh pasta has so much flavour that I'd happily serve it with just a little butter and some cheese because it's so delicious.

225g '00' flour, plus extra as required
  and for dusting
2 eggs
40g rose harissa
good pinch of Maldon sea salt flakes

SERVES 2–4

Put all the ingredients into a large bowl and mix. Gather the mixture into a ball using your hands, adding a little extra flour to bring it together if necessary (harissa varies from brand to brand, so you may need to add a little more flour if your dough is sticky). Knead the dough in the bowl for a few minutes, ensuring you pull and stretch it to activate the gluten in the flour, which gives the finished pasta a nice smooth texture. Put the dough into a clean bowl, cover with clingfilm and refrigerate for 30 minutes.

Set your pasta machine on a clean work surface and dust the rollers with '00' flour. Using a rolling pin, flatten the dough a little so that it will fit into the rollers of the pasta machine. Push the dough through the pasta first on the thickest setting, then repeat, each time on a thinner setting down to setting number 3 (any lower and the dough may stick). Once the pasta sheet is nice and thin, choose your preferred setting for either tagliatelle, linguine or spaghetti, then pass the pasta through once more to cut it into your chosen pasta shape.

To cook, bring a pan of salted water to the boil, add the pasta and cook for 2–3 minutes, or until al dente. Serve immediately with whatever you fancy.

LEMON & CUMIN PASTA DOUGH

I like to serve this pasta with crumbled feta and a healthy sprinkling of chilli flakes to top it off. This is heaven to me.

200g '00' flour, plus extra for dusting
2 eggs
1 teaspoon cumin seeds, toasted and
  finely ground
finely grated zest of 1 unwaxed lemon
½ small packet (about 15g) of fresh
  coriander, leaves very finely chopped
good pinch of sea salt flakes
½ teaspoon freshly ground black pepper

SERVES 2–4

Put all the ingredients into a large bowl and mix. Gather the mixture into a ball using your hands, adding a little extra flour to bring it together if necessary. Knead the dough in the bowl for a few minutes, ensuring you pull and stretch it to activate the gluten in the flour, which gives the finished pasta a nice smooth texture. Put the dough into a clean bowl, cover with clingfilm and refrigerate for 30 minutes.

Follow the method above to roll out and cook the pasta.

This pasta also works well with freshly cooked vegetables such as broccoli, peas, chard or spinach leaves.

AUBERGINES IN TOMATO & TAMARIND SAUCE

Aubergines seem to be the Middle East's most popular vegetable, and for me it can sometimes be tricky to come up with new and interesting ways of using them. This simple aubergine dish is almost a stew, and the delicious sauce is really comforting. Cooking it slowly concentrates the flavours, so start preparing your sauce as early as possible to make this dish special. While I am happy to eat it by itself, you can serve it with basmati rice or bread and maybe even a few halves of hard-boiled egg.

vegetable oil

2 large onions, halved and thinly sliced
    into half moons

1 garlic bulb, cloves peeled

1 teaspoon ground cinnamon

3 tablespoons thick unsweetened
    tamarind paste

2 x 400g cans chopped tomatoes

4 tablespoons clear honey

6 aubergines

Maldon sea salt flakes and freshly
    ground black pepper

SERVES 4–6

Add enough vegetable oil to coat the base of a large saucepan and set over a medium heat. Fry the onion for 8–10 minutes, or until browned but not burnt.

Add the garlic cloves to the saucepan along with the cinnamon and cook for a couple of minutes, until the garlic begins to soften. Stir in the tamarind, tomato and honey and season generously. Reduce the heat to low and simmer gently for 1 hour (or more), until the sauce is reduced a little, and has sweetened and intensified in flavour.

Meanwhile, cut each aubergine in half lengthways and remove the stem, then slice each piece lengthways into 4 wedges. Line a tray with a double layer of kitchen paper.

Pour enough vegetable oil into another large saucepan to fill to a depth of about 2.5cm. Heat the oil over a high heat, then add the aubergine wedges. Fry for 15 minutes, turning occasionally, until browned and cooked through. Remove with a slotted spoon and transfer to the paper-lined plate to drain. Pat with kitchen paper to absorb the excess oil.

Once the sauce is cooked, add the aubergine wedges to the sauce and carefully stir to ensure they are well coated. Heat through, then serve.

STUFFED COURGETTES

WITH PRESERVED LEMON, PINE NUTS & FETA

There is so much that can be done with the courgette. This is a great way to use them for something a bit more substantial – stuffing them with a bulgur wheat filling spiked with bags of flavour complements the courgette flesh beautifully. Serve them whole, or cut them into smaller portions if you have created a feast of several dishes.

100g bulgur wheat

4 large courgettes, halved lengthways

4 fat preserved lemons, finely chopped

1 small packet (30g) of flat leaf parsley, finely chopped

50g pine nuts

200g feta cheese, crumbled

1 teaspoon dried wild oregano

1 tablespoon garlic granules

finely grated zest of 1 unwaxed lemon

Maldon sea salt flakes and freshly ground black pepper

SERVES 4

Cook the bulgur wheat according to the packet instructions, then drain and rinse it in cold water. Leave to drain – you want it to be as dry as possible.

Preheat the oven to 240°C (220°C fan), Gas Mark 9. Line a large baking tray with baking paper.

Using a teaspoon, scoop out all the flesh from the courgette halves, being careful not to break the skins. Put the skins on the prepared baking tray. Finely chop the courgette flesh and put it into a large mixing bowl.

Add the preserved lemon, parsley, pine nuts, feta, oregano, garlic granules and lemon zest to the courgette flesh. Season with a little salt and a lot of pepper, then use your hands to mix until everything is well combined and the mixture feels moist. Divide the mixture into 8 portions. Heap one portion into one courgette skin and press down on the filling mixture to fill the cavity and compress it to really pack in the mixture. Repeat with the remaining portions of filling and courgette skins.

Bake for 20–25 minutes, or until the skins are soft and the filling mixture is cooked through and browning on top. Serve immediately.

VEGETABLE DOLMA

WITH FREEKEH, PINE NUTS & POMEGRANATE MOLASSES

One of my favourite things to eat in the world is dolma. This recipe has a delicious sweet-and-sour flavour that reminds me of my childhood. Make them in large batches, as they freeze well once cooked.

1 large onion

6–8 large white cabbage leaves (intact as much as possible)

3 peppers (any colour you like)

4–6 large vine tomatoes

olive oil

For the filling

vegetable oil

1 onion, finely chopped

1 teaspoon ground coriander

1 teaspoon ground cumin

1 teaspoon ground cinnamon

1 teaspoon chilli flakes (optional)

400g can chopped tomatoes

1 small packet (about 30g) of flat leaf parsley, finely chopped

200g freekeh

75g pine nuts

50ml pomegranate molasses

Maldon sea salt flakes and freshly ground black pepper

For the poaching liquid

200ml boiling water

50ml pomegranate molasses

50g caster sugar

SERVES 4–6

Preheat the oven to 200°C (180°C fan), Gas Mark 6.

First prepare the vegetables for stuffing. Heat a large saucepan over a high heat and fill it half full with boiling water. Make a single cut in the onion lengthways, as if you were cutting it in half, but stop when you reach the centre. Boil the cabbage leaves together with the whole onion for about 7 minutes, or until just starting to soften. Drain, then set aside until cool enough to handle. Carefully peel away the outer layers of the onion, keeping them intact (the cut you made earlier will help you remove the layers). Reserve the largest 4–6 layers for stuffing, then chop up the remaining onion and set it aside. Take the cooked cabbage leaves and cut out and discard the stalk from each leaf. Slice off the tops of the peppers carefully to create a lid for each pepper, then remove the seeds. Repeat the process with the tomatoes, but set aside the pulp and seeds to add to the filling.

Heat a drizzle of vegetable oil in a large frying pan set over a medium heat. Add the chopped onion and cook for 6–8 minutes, or until soft and beginning to turn golden. Stir in the reserved tomato pulp and seeds, the ground spices and the chilli flakes and stir-fry for 1–2 minutes. Now mix in the canned tomatoes and parsley. Season the mixture well with salt and pepper, then cook for a further couple of minutes. Remove the pan from the heat. Allow the mixture to cool a little, then add the freekeh, pine nuts and pomegranate molasses and mix well.

Stuff the peppers and tomatoes with the filling mixture, leaving a gap between the filling and the lids to allow the filling mixture to expand during cooking, then stand them carefully in a large ovenproof dish. Divide the remaining filling mixture between the cabbage leaves and onion shells – simply wrap and seal each cabbage leaf over the filling as best you can, and roll the onion around the filling as tightly as possible. Lay the stuffed onion and cabbage leaves in the dish.

Combine the ingredients for the poaching liquid in a jug and stir until the sugar dissolves. Pour the liquid into the dish, then drizzle olive oil generously over each dolma. Roast for 45–55 minutes, or until nicely browned. Leave to cool and serve at room temperature.

HARISSA BLACK BEAN RAGOUT

WITH BUTTERNUT SQUASH

OK, so this dish isn't much of a looker, but never judge a book by its cover. I could happily eat this for breakfast, lunch or dinner. Pile it on to toasted bread, top with an egg or just ladle it into a bowl and serve with a nice hunk of toasted bread: pure comfort.

olive oil

2 large onions, roughly chopped

2 teaspoons garlic granules

2 teaspoons ground cumin

1 teaspoon ground cinnamon

300g dried black beans

1.5 litres boiling water

800g butternut squash, peeled,
    deseeded and cut into rough
    2.5cm chunks

2 tablespoons rose harissa, plus extra
    to serve

Maldon sea salt flakes and freshly ground
    black pepper

Greek yogurt, to serve

SERVES 4–6

Heat a large saucepan over a medium-low heat and add enough olive oil to coat the base of the pan. Add the onion and cook for about 6–8 minutes, or until soft and translucent, without browning.

Add the garlic granules and spices, then stir in the beans, adding a little more oil if you feel you need more to coat the beans, and cook for about 5 minutes, stirring regularly, then season generously with salt and pepper.

Pour 1 litre of the boiling water into the saucepan and stir well. Reduce the heat to medium-low and simmer gently for 25–30 minutes.

Mix in the butternut squash pieces (adding them at this stage will make them pleasingly dark in colour when cooked), rose harissa and the remaining boiling water. Taste and adjust the seasoning if desired, then cook for a further 30 minutes, or until the butternut squash is cooked through. Stir a little harissa through some Greek yogurt and serve with the ragout.

VEGETABLE TRAY BAKE

Who doesn't love the ease and convenience of a tray bake? Chuck it all in, roast it and you're done. Some of the best things I've eaten were born out of ease and convenience, and this is one of those super-lazy, feed-everyone type of creations. A nice bit of goats' cheese with some great bread and a little salad on the side and I couldn't be happier.

1 aubergine, cut diagonally into
    5mm-thick slices
1 large courgette, cut diagonally into
    1cm-thick slices
1 red pepper, cored, deseeded and cut
    lengthways into 6 strips
1 yellow pepper, cored, deseeded and
    cut lengthways into 6 strips
2 potatoes (unpeeled), cut into
    5mm-thick slices
1 tablespoon dried wild oregano
1 tablespoon garlic granules
1 tablespoon cumin seeds
1 tablespoon chilli flakes (optional)
6 tablespoons olive oil
Maldon sea salt flakes and freshly
    ground black pepper

SERVES 4

Preheat your oven to its highest setting, preferably fan assisted. Line the largest baking tray you have with baking paper.

Put the vegetables, herbs and spices and the olive oil into a large mixing bowl, then season generously with salt and pepper. Use your hands to mix and coat the vegetables in the herbs, spices and oil.

Tip the vegetables into the prepared tray and spread them out. It's fine if some of them overlap, but do what you can to expose as much of their surfaces as possible. Roast for 16–18 minutes, or until the vegetables are cooked through and browned. Serve immediately.

POTATO, RICOTTA & HERB DUMPLINGS
WITH WALNUTS & PUL BIBER BUTTER

For me, this is perhaps one of the most comforting recipes in this book. I love the combination of cheese and potato – add melted butter and a spike of chilli heat and I'm in heaven. This recipe is inspired by a Transylvanian cheese and potato dumpling dish I once ate that has forever etched itself in my memory... sadly, I never got the recipe, so I came up with this one instead.

For the dumplings
750g potatoes
500g ricotta cheese, drained well
2 eggs
1 small packet (about 30g) of dill, finely chopped
50g '00' flour
light olive oil, for frying
Maldon sea salt flakes and freshly ground black pepper

For the sauce
125g salted butter
3 teaspoons pul biber chilli flakes
50g chopped walnuts

SERVES 4-6

Boil the potatoes whole for 25–35 minutes, or until cooked through. Drain and allow to cool slightly, then peel away the skins and mash them in a large mixing bowl while they are still warm. Leave to cool.

Once the mashed potato has cooled, add the ricotta, eggs, dill and flour and season generously with salt and pepper. Mix until evenly combined, then refrigerate for 30 minutes to firm up.

Shape the mixture into small dumplings a little larger than the size of your thumb. Dust each dumpling lightly with the flour and flatten slightly. Heat a frying pan over a medium-high heat and add a drizzle of light olive oil. Flash-fry the dumplings for just a few minutes – the outsides should be golden brown and the centres just warmed through.

To make sauce, melt the butter in a small saucepan over a low heat and stir in the pul biber and walnuts.

Once the butter is warm, transfer the dumplings to a warmed serving plate, pour over the walnut and chilli butter, then serve immediately.

STORE-CUPBOARD
SUSTENANCE

FETA, PUL BIBER & OREGANO MACARONI BAKE

I have so much love for 'mac and cheese' of every description – from the simple classic to the meaty Cypriot pastitsio, it's all good to me. This version was something I came up with for my neighbour Janet who loves her macaroni cheese and also enjoys spicy flavours, and not surprisingly, it is absolutely delicious and extremely comforting, too.

500g macaroni

2 heaped teaspoons pul biber chilli flakes

handful of oregano leaves, roughly chopped

finely grated zest of 1 unwaxed lemon

For the sauce

50g plain flour

50g salted butter

500ml full-fat milk

100g crème fraîche

400g feta cheese, crumbled (reserve a handful for the topping)

1 egg, beaten

2 teaspoons freshly ground black pepper

Maldon sea salt flakes

SERVES 6-8

First make the feta sauce. Heat a large saucepan over a medium-low heat. Add the flour and dry-toast for 1 minute, stirring constantly and bashing out any lumps with a wooden spoon. Add the butter and stir in the milk and crème fraîche, then whisk until the butter has melted, the milk is incorporated and the mixture is smooth. Add the feta and stir in, then remove from the heat and quickly stir in the beaten egg, the pepper and add a sprinkling of salt (bear in mind that the feta will be salty).

Preheat the oven to 220ºC (200ºC fan), Gas Mark 7. Select a large baking tray or ovenproof dish about 26 x 20cm.

Boil the macaroni according to the packet instructions, then drain the pasta and return it to the pan. Add the pul biber, oregano, lemon zest and feta sauce and mix well. Transfer the mixture to the baking tray or dish, then crumble over the reserved feta. Bake for 25 minutes, or until browning on top. Serve immediately.

LEMON, BLACK PEPPER, PECORINO & CABBAGE RICE

This is a controversial version of a risotto using basmati, which is a method I first spotted in a Gérard Depardieu cookbook many years ago. I won't say it is a better rice to use for risotto making, but I will say that I always have it in the house, so for me it is a convenient twist. I have taken my love of spaghetti cacio e pepe (with Pecorino and black pepper) as inspiration for this recipe, adding fresh lemon zest. There are also lovely ribbons of delicate cabbage leaves, which I think complement the rich, cheesy sauce perfectly.

olive oil

1 white onion, very finely chopped

300g basmati rice

100g butter

1.25–1.5 litres boiling water

1 teaspoon freshly ground black pepper
   (mill it coarsely)

100g pecorino cheese, finely grated,
   plus extra (optional) to serve

½ large Savoy cabbage, shredded
   into ribbons

finely grated zest of 1 unwaxed lemon

SERVES 4-6

Heat a large saucepan over a medium-low heat and add enough olive oil to coat the base of the pan. Add the onion and cook for about 8–10 minutes, or until soft and translucent, without browning.

Add the rice and half the butter to the saucepan and stir gently for a minute or so. Then begin adding the boiling water a ladleful at a time, stirring constantly, ensuring that each ladleful of water is absorbed before adding the next. Don't be tempted to increase the heat to speed up the process – you don't want the liquid to evaporate too quickly, as the rice won't cook properly. Once you have used one-third of the water, check the rice to see if it has cooked through (the grains should not be hard in the centre). Continue stirring and adding water this way until the rice is cooked to your liking.

Add the pepper and pecorino and stir rapidly to ensure the mixture becomes creamy and smooth. Now stir in the cabbage, followed by the remaining butter. Lastly, mix in the lemon zest. Take the pan off the heat and ladle the risotto into serving bowls. Drizzle a little olive oil over each serving, then scatter over some pecorino, if desired. Serve immediately.

HARISSA & SOBA NOODLE SALAD
WITH BROCCOLI, SESAME & NIGELLA SEEDS

The first time I tried Nigella Lawson's soba noodle salad, I fell head over heels in love. Although this version bears little similarity to the original, it remains a polite and respectful nod to the ever-inspiring Ms Lawson and her wonderful soba noodle salad, with the addition of a few Sabrina staples.

250g soba noodles

olive oil

300g Tenderstem broccoli, halved into
    2 lengths

50g sesame seeds, toasted

25g nigella seeds

For the dressing

2 tablespoons rose harissa

3 tablespoons tahini

1 fat garlic clove, crushed

juice of ½ lime

2 tablespoons clear honey

approximately 6 tablespoons
    lukewarm water

SERVES 4–6

Cook the soba noodles according to the packet instructions, then drain and rinse them under cold running water. Drain again, then set aside.

Heat a drizzle of olive oil in a frying pan over a medium-high heat. Rinse the broccoli stalks and florets, drain them briefly, then add them to the pan along with the residual water from rinsing. Sauté for a couple of minutes, stirring, then cover the pan with a lid and steam for 2–3 minutes. Remove the broccoli from the pan and set aside to cool.

Mix the ingredients for the dressing together in a bowl, adding only as much of the lukewarm water as you need – the sauce should be runny enough to coat all the noodles.

Put the noodles into a large mixing bowl. Pour over the dressing, then add the sesame and nigella seeds and the broccoli and toss well. Serve immediately.

ROASTED AUBERGINE & CARROT COUSCOUS
WITH PRESERVED LEMON

To all those people who say that couscous is bland, I say you just haven't tried the right recipe yet. Couscous should be used as a carrier for bold flavours, so if you're wondering what to do with a packet of it, try raiding your spice rack and store cupboard in search of strong flavours that will give character to your couscous-based meals. This tasty dish is delicious served either hot or cold, which means any leftovers are ideal for tomorrow's lunchboxes.

4 aubergines, cut into 2.5cm dice

extra virgin olive oil

6 small carrots, peeled and cut into batons

2 teaspoons dried wild oregano

2 teaspoons cumin seeds

300g couscous

2 teaspoons turmeric

1 teaspoon ground cinnamon

2 teaspoons ground coriander

2 fat garlic cloves, crushed

450ml hot water

4–5 preserved lemons, deseeded and finely chopped

1 small packet (about 30g) of dill, finely chopped

1 small packet (about 30g) of flat leaf parsley, finely chopped

Maldon sea salt flakes and freshly ground black pepper

SERVES 6-8

Preheat the oven to 220°C (200°C fan), Gas Mark 7. Line the largest baking tray you have, plus another baking tray, with baking paper.

Put the aubergine cubes into the largest prepared tray, season with pepper, drizzle over a generous amount of olive oil and place the tray on the higher shelf in the oven. Put the carrots into the other tray, season with salt, pepper and the oregano and drizzle with olive oil. Add to the oven and roast both trays for 25–30 minutes, until the aubergine is cooked through and browned, and the carrots are cooked and charred around the edges.

Toast the cumin seeds in a large, dry saucepan over a medium-high heat for 1 minute, then take the pan off the heat, add the couscous and allow it to toast briefly. Stir in the other spices, the crushed garlic and measured hot water with a generous amount of salt and pepper. Cover the saucepan with a lid (or use clingfilm) and set aside for 8–10 minutes to allow the couscous grains to absorb the liquid.

Once the liquid has been absorbed, use a fork to carefully fluff up the couscous. Now add the roasted aubergines and carrots, the preserved lemon and fresh herbs and fold them in carefully. Return to the heat briefly, if needed, and serve hot.

FREEKEH, PEA, FETA & SPRING ONION FRITTERS

Freekeh is wheat, harvested while still young and green, smoked and sometimes broken. So flavoursome, its somewhat grassy and nutty taste is delicious in salads, soups, pilafs and more. Here, I capitalize on its smoky flavour and chewy texture and combine it with the humble pea and some creamy, salty feta to make these wonderfully crisp and moreish fritters. A little yogurt on the side is a lovely addition.

vegetable oil, for frying

150g freekeh, boiled for 25 minutes, rinsed and drained until dry

5 spring onions, thinly sliced from root to tip

100g fresh peas

200g feta cheese, crumbled

1 tablespoon dried wild thyme

1 tablespoon pul biber chilli flakes

2 large eggs

6 tablespoons plain flour

Maldon sea salt flakes and freshly ground black pepper

Greek yogurt, to serve

MAKES 12–16

Pour enough vegetable oil into a large, deep frying pan or saucepan to fill to a depth of about 5cm. Heat the oil over a medium-high heat and bring to frying temperature (add a pinch of mixture: if it sizzles immediately, the oil is hot enough). Line a tray with a double layer of kitchen paper.

Combine the remaining ingredients in a large mixing bowl, seasoning well with salt and pepper. Mix using your hands for a few minutes until the mixture becomes easier to work.

When the oil is ready for frying, use 2 dessertspoons to form quenelles of the mixture: scoop up the mixture with one spoon and use the other to press down on the mixture to shape and compress it. Carefully lower the quenelles into the hot oil one at a time, as you make them, and fry in batches, for 3–4 minutes, or until deep golden brown all over. Remove the fritters from the oil with a slotted spoon and transfer to the paper-lined plate to drain. Sprinkle with salt flakes and serve immediately with Greek yogurt for dipping.

PEA, DILL & GARLIC RICE
WITH SAFFRON

This is my twist on the Persian classic baghala polow, a lovely aromatic dill and broad bean rice dish. This version uses simple, cost-effective and readily available frozen peas and I am very pleased with the results. The best news? No fiddly peeling of pods is necessary.

375g basmati rice

vegetable oil

1 large garlic bulb, cloves peeled and
    thinly sliced

generous pinch of saffron threads

100g dill, finely chopped

100g butter, cubed

400g frozen peas

Maldon sea salt flakes and freshly
    ground black pepper

SERVES 6–8

Cook the rice according to the packet instructions. Once cooked, drain and rinse under cold running water. Drain again, then set aside.

Heat a drizzle of vegetable oil in a large saucepan over a medium-low heat. Add the garlic and fry for 1–2 minutes, or until soft and translucent and it begins to turn golden around the edges.

Crumble in the saffron, breaking it down as much as possible, stir well, then add the dill and fry for a few minutes more, until the dill wilts. Season heavily with salt and pepper (add enough at this stage to season the peas and all the cooked rice) and mix well.

Stir the butter into the pan, allow it to melt, then add the cooked rice. Stir-fry for 2–3 minutes, then add the peas and cook for a few more minutes. Cover the pan with a lid and cook for a final 10–15 minutes. Taste and adjust the seasoning if necessary before serving.

SPICED GREEN BEAN & TOMATO RICE

I confess that I have done something no respectable Iranian should ever do: extract the meat from a much-loved Persian recipe classic, loobia polow (rice cooked with green beans and meat). But I am pleased to report that it is every bit as good as the original. We Iranians tend to embrace meat in everything, but the truth is that this vegetarian version has plenty going for it.

350g basmati rice

4–5 tablespoons ghee or vegetable oil

1 large onion, finely chopped

400g fine green beans, trimmed, each cut into 4 equal pieces

4 fat garlic cloves, thinly sliced

1 teaspoon turmeric

2 teaspoons ground cinnamon

4 tablespoons tomato purée

75g butter, cubed

1 tablespoon Greek yogurt

pinch of good-quality saffron threads, ground to a powder using a pestle and mortar, then steeped in 2–3 tablespoons boiling water until cool

Maldon sea salt flakes and freshly ground black pepper

SERVES 4–6

Bring a saucepan of water to the boil, add the rice and parboil for 6 minutes. Once parboiled, drain the rice in a sieve and rinse thoroughly under cold running water for a couple of minutes, using your fingers to wash off the starch. Shake vigorously to drain, then set aside.

Heat 2 tablespoons of the ghee or vegetable oil in a large frying pan over a medium heat. Add the onion and cook for 6–8 minutes, or until soft and translucent. Add the green beans, stir well and cook for 15–20 minutes, or until they are completely soft. Add the garlic and cook for a further 10–15 minutes. Mix in the turmeric and cinnamon, then season heavily with salt and pepper (be very generous, as this will need to season all the cooked rice, too). Once the garlic has softened, add the tomato purée, mix it in and cook for 5 minutes. Stir in the butter, then take the pan off the heat. Tip the rice into the green bean mixture and fold everything together gently, without breaking the rice grains, until evenly combined.

Select a large lidded saucepan and line the base with a disc of baking paper cut slightly larger than the base itself. Heat the pan over a low heat, add the remaining ghee or oil and allow it to melt over the paper. Stir the yogurt into the saffron solution, then add it to the melted ghee or oil and stir in quickly.

Scatter the green bean and rice mixture into the saucepan, pressing into the edges and base of the pan to create a flat bottom. Smooth the surface, then, using the handle of a wooden spoon, poke a series of holes into the rice, piercing all the way to the base of the pan (this allows the steam to circulate). Wrap the pan lid in a tea towel, cover the pan with the lid and cook over the lowest temperature for 45 minutes.

Once cooked, remove the lid, place a large platter over the saucepan and carefully flip the rice on to the plate to reveal the crunchy *tahdig* base. If it doesn't turn out perfectly, remove the crunchy base, slice it into portions and place it over the rice, as pictured.

MUSHROOM, TAHINI & HARISSA SPAGHETTI

In this dish the mushrooms are blitzed to a minced-meat consistency so it's easy to forget they are the key ingredient. This full-bodied, gratifying noodle dish draws inspiration from the dan dan noodles of the Sichuan province of China. You can make it as a dry noodle dish, or simply add water or milk to make it more of a soup.

handful of sesame seeds

½ teaspoon chilli flakes

1kg chestnut mushrooms

olive oil

6 fat garlic cloves, thinly sliced

1 heaped teaspoon ground cinnamon

2 teaspoons ground cumin

1 teaspoon coarsely ground black pepper

4 tablespoons light soy sauce, plus extra to taste

3 tablespoons rose harissa

2 tablespoons tahini

1 litre boiling water (or 500ml boiling water and 500ml milk)

400g spaghetti or egg noodles, cooked according to the packet instructions

1 bunch of spring onions, thinly sliced diagonally from root to tip

1 small packet (about 30g) of fresh coriander, roughly chopped

Maldon sea salt flakes

SERVES 4–6

Toast the sesame seeds and chilli flakes in a small, dry frying pan over a medium heat for 2–3 minutes, or until they release their aroma. Remove from the heat and set aside.

Put the mushrooms into the bowl of a food processor and pulse until roughly blitzed, ensuring not to over-process. Alternatively, chop the mushrooms finely by hand.

Heat a wok or large saucepan over a high heat. Add the chopped mushrooms to the dry pan and fry for 5–6 minutes, or until they have released some moisture and are nicely browned. Add a drizzle of olive oil to the pan, reduce the heat to medium, then add the garlic and fry for 2 minutes, or until it is translucent.

Add the cinnamon, cumin and pepper to the pan and fry for 2 minutes. Now mix in the soy sauce, harissa and tahini. Stir in the boiling water as desired (and milk, if using), depending on whether you want just enough sauce to coat all the noodles, or more of a soup. Season with salt and extra soy sauce to taste, then increase the heat and bring to the boil. Stir in the cooked noodles, spring onion and coriander, and as soon as the noodles have heated through, serve with the toasted sesame seeds and chilli flakes sprinkled on top.

SPAGHETTI WITH OLIVES, BROCCOLI & FETA

I am obsessed with adding greens to pasta dishes – broccoli and cabbage are usually my favourites, and both work well in this recipe. I always keep feta in my refrigerator, and usually have olives of some description in a corner of my cupboard, both of which are great to throw into a tangle of pasta to add a tangy bite of flavour. It doesn't really matter which type of pasta you use – I grab whatever I have to hand. I always make a big batch of this dish, and sometimes I end up eating leftovers cold for breakfast – but that really is another story.

olive oil

1 large garlic bulb, cloves peeled and thinly sliced

500g spaghetti or linguine

300g broccoli, cut into florets

150g pitted black olives or mixed olives, halved or roughly chopped

2–3 tablespoons pul biber

finely grated zest of 2 unwaxed lemons

400g feta cheese, crumbled

Maldon sea salt flakes and freshly ground black pepper

SERVES 4–6

Bring a large saucepan of water to the boil over a high heat and season it well with salt.

Meanwhile, heat another large saucepan over a medium-low heat and add enough olive oil to coat the base of the pan. Add the garlic and cook for about 6–8 minutes, or until soft and translucent, without browning. Remove from the heat.

Add the pasta to the boiling water and cook according to the packet instructions. Once half the cooking time for the pasta has elapsed, set the pan containing the garlic back on the hob over a medium-high heat and add the broccoli. Stir-fry for the few remaining minutes needed to cook the pasta.

Using tongs, lift the pasta from the water and add it to the broccoli pan along with a few spoonfuls of the pasta cooking water. Stir well, then add a good drizzle of olive oil and a generous seasoning of salt and black pepper. Add the olives, pul biber and lemon zest and combine, then add the feta and toss the pasta well to evenly distribute the ingredients. If the dish seems a little dry, mix in some more of the pasta water. Serve immediately.

SPECTACULAR SIDES

SHALLOT BLOSSOMS

WITH PAPRIKA CRÈME FRAÎCHE

I first tried a version of these at a restaurant on holiday in the States many moons ago – we loved them so much, we ordered plate after plate! My version here is every bit as delicious, and can be served as finger food or as a nice addition to a meal. The dip is a simple yet perfect accompaniment.

vegetable oil, for frying

450g long shallots, peeled but
    kept whole

100g plain flour

1 tablespoon paprika

1 tablespoon garlic granules

1 tablespoon dried wild oregano

2 teaspoons celery salt

1 teaspoon cayenne pepper

1 large egg, beaten

For the dip

200g crème fraîche

2 teaspoons paprika

Maldon sea salt flakes and freshly
    ground black pepper

SERVES 4

To make the dip, mix the crème fraîche and paprika in a bowl and season with a generous amount of salt and pepper. Refrigerate until ready to serve.

Pour enough vegetable oil into a large, deep frying pan or saucepan to fill to a depth of about 5cm. Heat the oil over a medium-high heat and bring to frying temperature (add a pinch of the batter mixture: if it sizzles immediately, the oil is hot enough). Line a plate with a double layer of kitchen paper.

Meanwhile, cut off the root from the shallots. Cutting through the root end towards the tip, make about 8 cuts into each shallot to create matchstick-sized 'petals', stopping 1cm from the tip so that the shallot stays intact. Gently separate out the cut ends of each shallot.

Put the flour, paprika, garlic granules, celery salt and cayenne pepper into a deep plastic container and mix well. Put the beaten egg into a separate bowl.

When the oil is at frying temperature, dip a shallot into the spiced flour and shake it around to coat all the edges in the flour. Shake off any excess flour, then dip it immediately into the beaten egg, again doing your best to coat the insides. Shake off any excess egg, then return the shallot to the spiced flour and coat a second time in the flour. Carefully lower the coated shallot into the hot oil. Repeat with the remaining shallots. Fry for 2–3 minutes, turning halfway, until all sides are deep golden brown. Remove from the oil using a slotted spoon and transfer to the paper-lined plate to drain. Serve hot, sprinkled with extra salt flakes and with the dip on the side.

CRUMBED ASPARAGUS
WITH SAFFRON YOGURT

The closest thing I've ever had to this dish was asparagus tempura, and I remember thinking what a complete joy it was. This version is crumbed instead of battered, which helps retain a wonderful texture. The saffron yogurt is my version of an aioli but, of course, Middle Eastern style.

vegetable oil, for frying

1 large egg, beaten

1 heaped tablespoon garlic granules

75g fine white breadcrumbs

150g asparagus spears, woody ends
  trimmed off

Maldon sea salt flakes and freshly ground
  black pepper

For the saffron yogurt

pinch of saffron threads, ground to
  a powder using a pestle and mortar

1 tablespoon boiling water

200g Greek yogurt

1 small garlic clove (or ½ fat one),
  crushed

Maldon sea salt flakes and freshly
  ground black pepper

SERVES 4

To make the saffron yogurt, put the saffron threads into a small cup and pour over the measured boiling water. Gently swirl the mixture and then leave to steep until the liquid is cool. Stir the saffron solution into the Greek yogurt, add the garlic and a generous amount of salt and pepper and mix well. Refrigerate until ready to serve.

Pour enough vegetable oil into a large, deep frying pan or saucepan to fill to a depth of about 5cm. Heat the oil over a medium-high heat and bring to frying temperature (add a pinch of the breadcrumb mixture: if it sizzles immediately, the oil is hot enough). Line a plate with a double layer of kitchen paper.

Meanwhile, put the beaten egg, garlic granules and a generous amount of salt and pepper into a shallow bowl and mix well until the mixture is as smooth as possible. Put the breadcrumbs on a plate.

When the oil is at frying temperature, dip an asparagus spear into the beaten egg to coat, then roll it in the breadcrumbs. Now immediately lower the breaded asparagus carefully into the hot oil and fry for a few minutes, until golden brown all over. Repeat with the remaining asparagus, but do not overcrowd the pan – fry in batches if necessary. Remove the asparagus carefully using a slotted spoon or metal tongs and transfer to the paper-lined plate to drain. Serve hot, sprinkled with extra salt flakes and with the saffron yogurt on the side.

CHARGRILLED SPRING ONIONS
WITH HAZELNUTS & LIME & HONEY DRESSING

I love spring onions – in everything, on everything and with everything. Traditionally we eat them raw with bread and feta cheese as staple fare of the Persian table. Grilling them mellows out the oniony flavour, and intense charring works beautifully with the sweetness of cooked onion flesh. Chargrilling them on a barbecue is ideal, but you can also cook them easily on the hob in a griddle pan. The dressing for this delicious salad combines well with the grilled onion, and the toasted hazelnuts add a satisfying crunch. This dish is great served alone or as an accompaniment at any time of year.

30g blanched hazelnuts

12 spring onions

For the dressing

1½ tablespoons olive oil

juice of ½ fat lime

1 tablespoon clear honey

Maldon sea salt flakes and freshly
  ground black pepper

To garnish

2 pinches of pul biber chilli flakes

finely grated zest of ½ unwaxed lime

SERVES 4–6

First make the dressing. Combine the olive oil, lime juice, honey and a good amount of salt and pepper in a small bowl or jug and set aside.

Toast the hazelnuts in a dry frying pan set over a medium-high heat until charred but not burnt. Set aside until cool enough to handle, then roughly halve or chop them.

Meanwhile, bring some water to the boil in a saucepan. Blanch the spring onions in the boiling water for 2 minutes, then drain and dry them well with kitchen paper. Meanwhile, preheat a griddle pan over a high heat. Arrange the blanched spring onions on the griddle pan and chargrill for a few minutes on each side, until char marks appear.

Arrange the spring onions on a serving plate and scatter over the hazelnuts. Drizzle the dressing over the spring onions. Sprinkle over the pul biber and grated lime zest, then serve.

STIR-FRIED CAVOLO NERO, CHESTNUTS, MUSHROOMS & CHICKPEAS

I first made this warm salad back in my supperclub days, when I had an unannounced vegan guest. Thankfully, a well-stocked refrigerator and a can of chickpeas proved to be my saviour. My guest loved this dish so much, I began serving it regularly as an autumnal vegan offering. It really is quite delicious.

500g chestnut mushrooms, chopped

2 tablespoons garlic oil

1 teaspoon ground cumin

½ teaspoon turmeric

½ teaspoon ground cinnamon

½ teaspoon cayenne pepper

generous pinch of Maldon sea salt flakes

250g cavolo nero, tough stalks discarded, roughly chopped

10–12 vacuum-packed cooked chestnuts, halved

400g can chickpeas, drained and rinsed

SERVES 4–6

Heat a large saucepan over a high heat until hot, then add the mushrooms to the dry pan and cook for 6–8 minutes, stirring a couple of times only, until any moisture has evaporated. Reduce the heat, then add the garlic oil, spices and salt.

Add the cavolo nero to the saucepan and stir-fry for 1 minute, then mix in the halved chestnuts and chickpeas and cook for another couple of minutes, until the cavolo nero has wilted and is cooked – it should retain some bite. Serve immediately.

GARLIC & CHILLI MASHED BUTTERNUT SQUASH

I don't think I have ever come across a butternut squash dish I didn't like. This is definitely one of my favourites, and it makes a perfect side dish – but if I'm in the right mood, no one can stop me from devouring it on its own.

2 x 1kg butternut squash (unpeeled)

olive oil

2 fat garlic cloves, crushed

1 teaspoon chilli flakes

generous knob of butter

2 tablespoons tahini

2 pinches of sumac

handful of pine nuts

Maldon sea salt flakes and freshly
    ground black pepper

SERVES 4–6

Preheat the oven to 200°C (180°C fan), Gas Mark 6.

Cut the butternut squashes in half lengthways and scoop out and discard the seeds. Drizzle each squash half with olive oil and rub the oil across the flesh. Place the squash on a baking tray and roast for 1 hour, or until the flesh is soft and cooked through.

Remove the roasted squash halves from the oven and set them on a chopping board. Use a spoon to scoop out the flesh and place it in a mixing bowl, discarding the skins. Add the garlic and chilli flakes and mash the squash until smooth, then add the butter and mix well. Transfer the mashed squash to a saucepan and set the pan over a medium heat. Cook the squash for 5 minutes, stirring occasionally.

Transfer the butternut mash to a large, wide serving platter and spread it out to the edges of the platter. Drizzle over the tahini, sprinkle over the sumac and scatter over the pine nuts. Finish with a drizzle of olive oil, then serve immediately.

CELERIAC & HARISSA BAKE

I have a strange love for the smell of cut raw celeriac – its subtle, citrusy notes send me into a frenzy. While we have the French to thank for the marvellous celeriac remoulade, and we do occasionally use celeriac to make purées, I think this is another of those greatly underused vegetables. With a little harissa magic, it makes for the most wonderful baked dish – its natural flavour standing up well against the spice of the harissa.

750g celeriac, peeled

2 tablespoons clear honey

2 tablespoons good-quality vegetable
   stock powder

2 tablespoons harissa

approximately 400ml boiling water

SERVES 6-8

Preheat the oven to 220°C (200°C fan), Gas Mark 7. Select a round ovenproof dish roughly 20cm in diameter.

Slice the celeriac into 3 equally thick discs, then cut each slice in half. Thinly slice each piece. Arrange the sliced celeriac in the dish.

Put the honey, stock and harissa into a measuring jug and pour over enough boiling water to bring the liquid level up to 400ml. Stir well, then pour the mixture over the celeriac. Bake for 40–45 minutes, or until the celeriac is cooked through. Halfway through the cooking time, use a spoon to baste the celeriac and push it down into the sauce, then return the dish to the oven to finish cooking. Serve immediately.

ROASTED PARSNIPS
WITH HARISSA ORANGE GLAZE

Growing up in England has meant that parsnips have played an important role in our home cooking and I couldn't imagine a Christmas meal without them. I like to roast them with just salt and pepper and dip them into horseradish cream, and I adore them in cakes, because their natural sweetness is really something special. This recipe is a sticky, chewy, spicy, sweet revelation. I challenge you not to eat half of it before it even hits the table!

1kg parsnips

olive oil

Maldon sea salt flakes and freshly
   ground black pepper

For the glaze

3 tablespoons clear honey

2 tablespoons rose harissa

finely grated zest and juice of
   1 unwaxed orange

SERVES 4–6

Preheat the oven to 220°C (200°C fan), Gas Mark 7. Line the largest roasting dish you have with baking paper.

Mix the glaze ingredients together in a small bowl and set aside.

Peel the parsnips and cut them roughly into 2.5cm-thick pieces about 5cm long – don't worry about being too precise, just make them all roughly the same size. Put them into the roasting dish, drizzle with olive oil and season well with salt and pepper. Roast for 30 minutes, or until cooked through and slightly brown.

Pour the glaze over the parsnips, toss well and roast for a further 10–12 minutes. Remove the dish from the oven, then stir the parsnip pieces in the glaze before serving.

SPICED SWEET POTATO & ONION HASH

This kind of one-pan dish is literally my go-to recipe when I'm craving something simple but effective. If you wanted to make it any more satisfying, or bulk it up to serve two for brunch, then an egg on top – fried or poached – is the perfect pairing.

vegetable oil, for frying

2 large slices of sourdough bread, cut into rough cubes

1 small packet (about 30g) of flat leaf parsley, roughly chopped

500g sweet potatoes, peeled and cut into cubes

1 teaspoon black mustard seeds

2 teaspoons coriander seeds

1 onion, roughly chopped

2 garlic cloves, bashed

Maldon sea salt flakes and freshly ground black pepper

SERVES 2–4

Heat a frying pan over a medium heat and add a generous drizzle of vegetable oil. Add the bread cubes, season generously with salt and pepper and stir well. Cook for about 5 minutes, or until the bread is browned. Remove the pan from the heat, stir in the chopped parsley and set aside.

Heat a separate large frying pan over a medium heat and drizzle in enough oil to generously coat the base of the pan. Add the sweet potato and cook, turning frequently, for 30 minutes, or until the potato begins to soften.

Add the mustard and coriander seeds and onion to the pan and cook, stirring, for 1 minute, or until the seeds start to pop. Add the garlic and stir, ensuring everything is coated in the seeds. Cook for 1–2 minutes, or until the garlic has softened.

Tip the bread cubes into the pan with the sweet potato. Mix everything together, then serve.

TARUNIMA'S OKRA FRIES

My friend Tarunima makes the most gorgeous and delicious cakes I've ever tasted – and not only that, but pretty much everything she creates has so much flavour that it's hard to control yourself when she's cooking for you. Her spiced okra fries may well be my favourite type of fries of all. Even though my recipe isn't exactly the same as Tarunima's, it is still pretty darn fantastic. If you haven't tried spiced okra fries, you really haven't lived!

vegetable oil, for frying

2 teaspoons garlic granules

1 heaped teaspoon chilli powder

2 teaspoons turmeric

4 tablespoons chickpea (gram) flour

2 tablespoons cornflour

350g okra, each pod quartered
   lengthways

Maldon sea salt flakes and freshly
   ground black pepper

SERVES 4–6

Pour enough vegetable oil into a large, deep frying pan or saucepan to fill to a depth of about 5cm. Heat the oil over a medium-high heat and bring to frying temperature (add a small piece of okra: if it sizzles immediately, the oil is hot enough). Line a plate with a double layer of kitchen paper.

Meanwhile, combine the garlic granules, spices and flours in a large mixing bowl and season with salt and pepper. Add the okra and mix well to ensure the okra strips are well coated – add a few teaspoons of water if necessary to help the mixture to stick to the okra. Using your hands, coat the okra all over in the mixture.

When the oil is ready for deep-frying, carefully lower the strips, a few at a time, into the oil. Do not overcrowd the pan – cook in batches if necessary. Fry for about 6–8 minutes, until crisp and golden. Remove the okra fries using a slotted spoon and transfer to the paper-lined plate to drain. Sprinkle with salt flakes and serve immediately.

SWEET POTATO, COCONUT & THYME BAKE

Dauphinoise potatoes are one of my favourite things. This is a variation of that classic, employing Jamaican-inspired flavours found in rice and peas, and my love for sweet potatoes. I promise you, this dish is incredibly moreish.

750g sweet potatoes, peeled

2 fat garlic cloves, thinly sliced

4–5 sprigs of thyme, leaves picked and roughly chopped, reserving some for garnish

400ml can full-fat coconut milk

Maldon sea salt flakes and freshly ground black pepper

SERVES 6–8

Preheat the oven to 220°C (200°C fan), Gas Mark 7. Select a large baking tray or ovenproof dish about 26 x 20cm.

Using a mandoline slicer or a food processor slicing attachment set to a medium thickness, thinly slice the sweet potatoes. Alternatively, thinly slice by hand.

Use one-quarter of the sweet potatoes to create an overlapping layer in the base of the baking tray or dish. Distribute one-third of the garlic and thyme over the potato layer and season generously with salt and pepper. Repeat this layering process, finishing with a layer of sweet potato slices. Pour over the coconut milk, then gently press down on the contents of the dish with a spatula to compress, season with salt and pepper and sprinkle with the reserved thyme.

Bake for 20 minutes, then press down on the potato slices with the spatula to submerge them in the coconut milk. Return the dish to the oven and bake for a further 20–25 minutes. Serve immediately.

TEMPURA SPRING ONIONS

WITH HARISSA KETCHUP

You could coat a shoe in tempura batter and I'd probably love it. There is something endlessly satisfying about the ludicrously crunchy yet light coating, and it works beautifully with anything, from seafood to vegetables. For this dish I chose spring onion – they are always available and their sweetness only intensifies when cooked. They're perfect with my sweet and spicy harissa ketchup dip on the side.

vegetable oil, for frying
12 spring onions

For the harissa ketchup
100ml tomato ketchup
2 tablespoons rose harissa

For the tempura batter
1 large egg
125g plain flour
200ml ice-cold water
ice cubes

SERVES 4–6

Pour enough vegetable oil into a large, deep frying pan or saucepan to fill to a depth of about 5cm. Heat the oil over a medium-high heat and bring to frying temperature (add a teaspoon of batter: if it sizzles immediately, the oil is hot enough). Line a plate with a double layer of kitchen paper.

To make the harissa ketchup, combine the ketchup and harissa in a bowl. Set aside.

Crack the egg into a large mixing bowl and add the flour, but do not mix together. Have your iced water ready (add ice cubes to help keep it cold, but ensure they don't end up in the batter).

When the oil is ready for frying, pour the iced water into the bowl with the egg and flour and, using chopsticks or the handle of a wooden spoon (not a whisk), mix the flour, egg and water together quickly, until most of the flour is dissolved – ensure you don't overbeat the mixture.

Dip the spring onions, one at a time, into the batter to coat them well, then immediately transfer carefully into the hot oil. Fry in batches for 2–3 minutes, until the batter is crisp (it won't turn brown). Using a slotted spoon or metal tongs, remove the spring onions, shake off the excess oil and transfer to the paper-lined plate to drain. Sprinkle with salt flakes and serve immediately with the harissa ketchup.

KAFFIR LIME & SPICE-ROASTED CHICKPEAS

I'm a nibbler and a picker – if you leave little plates of food in front of me, I will happily graze on them instead of having a proper meal. This dish is packed full of flavour and great served hot or cold, alone or tossed into a salad of any kind to add more dimension. As I've always maintained, feta makes everything better, so a little crumbled feta cheese would be a heavenly addition, but is by no means necessary.

2 x 400g cans chickpeas, drained

1 teaspoon medium curry powder

1 teaspoon paprika

1 teaspoon turmeric

1 teaspoon ground cinnamon

1 teaspoon ground cumin

8 kaffir lime leaves

1 teaspoon ground fenugreek

2 teaspoons dried mint

2 fat garlic cloves, crushed

juice of ½ fat lime

2 tablespoons olive oil

generous amount of Maldon sea salt
   flakes and freshly ground black pepper

SERVES 4–6

Preheat oven to 220°C (200°C fan), Gas Mark 7. Line a baking tray with baking paper.

Put all the ingredients into a large mixing bowl and mix well, ensuring the chickpeas are well coated in the spiced oil. Tip the mixture into the prepared tray and roast for 20 minutes, stirring and turning the chickpeas once halfway through the cooking time. Serve immediately.

ROASTED NEW POTATOES WITH SPICED CITRUS BUTTER

This is a simple way of adding a kick of flavour to roasted new potatoes. Essentially, the magic comes from the spiced butter that contains sumac – which works brilliantly with many other vegetables, too. You'll be surprised at the versatility of sumac, and hopefully this recipe shows you one more way in which to use this mild citrusy spice.

750g new potatoes (unpeeled), halved
    lengthways
olive oil
Maldon sea salt flakes and freshly
    ground black pepper

For the spiced butter
50g salted butter, softened
2 teaspoons sumac
finely grated zest of 1 unwaxed orange
finely grated zest of 1 unwaxed lime
1 heaped teaspoon pul biber chilli flakes
2 garlic cloves, crushed
Maldon sea salt flakes and freshly
    ground black pepper

SERVES 4–6

First make the spiced butter. Put all the ingredients into a mixing bowl and season well with salt and pepper, then beat together with a wooden spoon. Lay out a sheet of clingfilm and spoon the butter into the centre. Wrap the clingfilm over the butter and form it into a log shape, twisting the ends closed to tighten and seal the butter inside (like a sweet in a wrapper). Refrigerate until needed.

Preheat the oven to 220°C (200°C fan), Gas Mark 7. Line a baking tray with baking paper. Place the halved potatoes in the prepared baking tray with their cut sides facing up. Drizzle generously with olive oil and season well with salt and pepper. Roast for 35 minutes, or until cooked through and nicely browned.

Remove the spiced butter from the refrigerator and cut it into small cubes. Scatter these over the potatoes, then roast for a further 5 minutes, until the butter has melted. Remove from oven, toss the potatoes to coat them well in the melted butter and serve immediately.

SPICED POTATO RÖSTI

There are few things in life better than fried potatoes, and I like to take them to the next level by adding a little spice. Serving yogurt, flavoured with my Sabzi Sauce, and a poached egg on the side transforms this into a spectacular side or main dish.

1kg new potatoes (or any waxy potato), unpeeled and coarsely grated

1 teaspoon cumin seeds

1 teaspoon black mustard seeds

1 teaspoon coriander seeds

1 teaspoon chilli flakes

1 teaspoon garlic granules

1 small packet (about 30g) of dill, finely chopped

3–4 tablespoons ghee

2 tablespoons Sabzi Sauce (*see* page 195)

100g Greek yogurt

Maldon sea salt flakes and freshly ground black pepper

For the eggs (optional)

olive oil, for greasing

4 eggs

SERVES 2–4

Put the grated potato into a large mixing bowl and season generously with salt (be generous, as this will be extracted later). Mix well and set aside for 10 minutes.

Once the salting time has elapsed, stir the potato again, then tip it out of the bowl on to a piece of muslin or a clean tea towel, or into a sieve, and squeeze the excess moisture from the potato. Put the potato into a clean bowl, add the spices, garlic granules and dill and season generously with black pepper. Mix well with a fork until all the ingredients are evenly combined (avoid mixing with your hands, as you run the risk of releasing more moisture from the potato).

Heat a large, nonstick frying pan, about 26cm in diameter, over a medium-low heat. Add the ghee to the pan, and once hot, scatter the potato mixture evenly into the pan. Using a spatula, flatten and smooth the surface of the mixture, pressing down gently. Cook for 8 minutes, then carefully check to see if the base has turned a deep golden brown – continue cooking for a further 2 minutes if necessary. Once the base has turned golden brown, carefully flip over the rösti and cook the other side for 8 minutes. If you're worried about turning it without breaking it, my tip is to place a plate over the frying pan, flip the whole thing on to the plate, then slide the rösti back into the pan to cook the other side.

If serving with poached eggs, bring a saucepan of water to a simmer. Line 4 small bowls or tea cups with clingfilm, rub the clingfilm with a little olive oil and crack an egg into each. Gather up the clingfilm around each raw egg, expelling any air, and twist it to seal. Tie each egg parcel closed with some kitchen string. Lower the egg parcels into the pan of boiling water and poach for 2–5 minutes, or until cooked to your liking. Use a slotted spoon to remove the parcels from the water.

Mix the Sabzi Sauce together with the yogurt. Serve with the rösti with the green yogurt and the poached eggs (if using).

'SHAKEN' SWEET QUICK-PICKLED ONIONS

I'm completely addicted to these onions and make them quite often, especially since they are ridiculously easy to prepare. Pile into cheese toasties or sandwiches, toss them into salads or serve with curries, stews and soups.

1 large red onion, halved and very thinly sliced into half moons

1 tablespoon caster sugar

1 tablespoon rice vinegar

1 teaspoon pul biber chilli flakes

generous amount of Maldon sea salt flakes

MAKES A SMALL BOWLFUL

Combine all the ingredients in a lidded plastic container. Close the lid tightly and shake vigorously for a couple of minutes until the onion slices soften, then serve. Keep refrigerated for up to 2 days in a sealed container.

SMACKED CUCUMBER SALAD

Cucumbers are a much-loved Persian staple and we eat them by the kilo. I wrote this recipe to appease my mother and her mad love for all things cucumber, so it features regularly in our house because it's so easy to make and such a great accompaniment to many dishes.

1 tablespoon sesame seeds

1 large cucumber, bashed all over against a hard surface or with a rolling pin, then cut into batons or chunks

Maldon sea salt flakes

For the dressing

1 teaspoon coriander seeds

1 teaspoon sesame oil

1 tablespoon rose harissa

2 tablespoons clear honey

1 tablespoon rice vinegar

1 garlic clove, crushed

1 teaspoon nigella seeds

squeeze of lemon juice

SERVES 2–4

Toast the sesame seeds in a dry frying pan over a medium-low heat for 4–5 minutes until browned, then remove from the heat and transfer to a bowl.

Put the coriander seeds for the dressing into the same pan and toast for about 1 minute, until they release their aroma. Remove from the heat, transfer to a pestle and mortar and crush them lightly, grinding just enough to crack the seeds.

To make the dressing, mix the sesame oil, harissa, honey, vinegar and garlic in a small bowl. Add the crushed coriander seeds, the nigella seeds and lemon juice and mix well.

Place the cucumber in a serving bowl, pour over the dressing, season with salt and, lastly, sprinkle over the toasted sesame seeds. Stir and serve.

SABZI SAUCE

Sabzi, the Persian word for herbs, is derived from the Persian word sabz, meaning green. This great little herby sauce is so versatile. Stir it into yogurt, use it to marinate halloumi, paneer or feta, or as a salad dressing, dollop it on to soups or in stews or smear it on to toasted flatbreads and top with feta cheese and chilli flakes for a snack... You get the drift – you can use it in everything!

50g flat leaf parsley, roughly chopped

50g dill, roughly chopped

25g chives, roughly chopped or snipped

50g fresh coriander, roughly chopped

1 long red chilli, deseeded if preferred

2 preserved lemons

1 tablespoon ground cumin

1 tablespoon ground coriander

1 fat garlic clove, crushed

200ml olive oil

Maldon sea salt flakes and freshly
    ground black pepper

MAKES 1 JAR

Using a food processor or blender, blitz all the ingredients until the mixture is smooth.

Transfer the mixture to an airtight food container or, for a longer life, a sterilized jar, and store in the refrigerator for up to 1 week – the colour may fade the longer you keep it, but this will not affect the taste.

SWEET TREATS

BEETROOT HALVA TART
WITH PISTACHIO NUTS

This is my take on the classic Indian dessert of gajar ka halwa – a painstakingly slow-cooked dessert made with grated carrots, spices, ghee and milk. I once tried something similar but with beetroot, which is how I came up with this version. It isn't as sweet, as I prefer to let the natural flavours of the beetroot do the talking.

For the filling

100g unsalted butter

2 teaspoons ground cinnamon

seeds from 8 cardamom pods, finely
    ground using a pestle and mortar

1kg raw beetroot, peeled and grated

250g caster sugar

300ml milk

50g pistachio nuts, roughly chopped

For the pastry

250g plain flour, plus extra for dusting

125g unsalted butter, softened

pinch of Maldon sea salt flakes

30g caster sugar

1 egg, beaten

1 egg yolk

SERVES 8-10

First make the filling. Melt the butter in a large saucepan over a medium heat, then add the spices. Stir for 30 seconds, then add the beetroot and sugar and mix well. Cook for about 5 minutes, or until the beetroot is soft. Pour in the milk and stir well, then lower the heat and simmer for 30–45 minutes, stirring occasionally to prevent burning, until all the liquid has been absorbed by the beetroot. This process does take time, so be patient. Once all the liquid has been absorbed, allow the mixture to cool, then refrigerate it for at least 1 hour.

Next make the pastry. Put the flour, butter, salt and sugar into a bowl and rub everything together with your fingertips, lifting the flour upwards from the base of the bowl, until the mixture resembles sand. Then make a well in the centre, add the egg and egg yolk and incorporate them into the flour mixture to form a smooth ball of dough.

Select a 24cm-diameter tart tin. Tear a large square of clingfilm and place it on your work surface. Dust generously with flour, then set the pastry dough on top, dust that with flour and cover it loosely with another layer of clingfilm. Using a rolling pin, roll out the dough until it is slightly larger than your tin. Remove the top layer of clingfilm and carefully transfer the dough into the tin. Push the dough gently into the edges of the tin, leaving a little overhanging. Now sweep the rolling pin across the top of the tin to cut off the overhanging dough. Cover with clingfilm and refrigerate for at least 30 minutes (or overnight).

Preheat the oven to 180°C (160°C fan), Gas Mark 4.

Remove the pastry case and the beetroot mixture from the refrigerator. Pour the beetroot mixture into the pastry case. If you have one, transfer the tin on to a pizza stone, then bake for 40–45 minutes, or until the pastry edges are crisp. Scatter the pistachios on top and gently press into the filling, then leave in the tin to cool completely before serving.

CINNAMON PAVLOVA
WITH SWEET LABNEH CREAM

Meringues are ideal after a heavy meal, because they feel a lot lighter and more digestible than many other desserts (or so I keep telling myself!). I use sweetened labneh and cream which really changes the character of a classic pavlova to something a bit different. The cinnamon meringue works beautifully with the figs, and Greek basil adds a refreshing touch.

For the meringue

6 large egg whites

300g caster sugar

1 heaped teaspoon ground cinnamon

1 tablespoon cornflour

1 teaspoon red wine vinegar

For the topping

600ml double cream

2 teaspoons vanilla bean paste

100g labneh

6 fat black figs, quartered

75g pistachio nut slithers (or roughly
    chopped whole nuts)

2–3 tablespoons clear honey

handful of Greek basil

handful of mint, leaves picked, rolled up
    tightly and thinly sliced into ribbons

SERVES 8–10

Preheat the oven to 160ºC (140ºC fan), Gas Mark 3. Select the largest baking sheet you have. Line it with baking paper, then draw a 24cm-diameter circle in the centre of the paper. Turn the paper over and you should still be able to see the circle, which you can use as a guide.

Using an electric hand whisk, whisk the egg whites in a large mixing bowl until stiff peaks form, then slowly add the sugar, 1 tablespoon at a time, until it is all incorporated into the egg white. Add the cinnamon, cornflour and vinegar and continue to whisk until they are well incorporated and the mixture is shiny and dense.

Fill the circle on the prepared baking sheet with the meringue mixture, then use a spatula to create peaks around the sides.

Transfer the baking sheet to the oven. Immediately reduce the temperature to 150ºC (130ºC fan), Gas Mark 2, and bake for 1½ hours, or until the meringue is cooked and crisp on the outside. Remove from oven and leave to cool completely.

Make the topping when you are ready to serve it. Using an electric hand whisk, whip the cream with the vanilla bean paste in a large mixing bowl until stiff peaks form. Once the cream is nice and firm, but not over-beaten, gently fold in the labneh.

Spread the cream over the meringue, then arrange the figs on top. Scatter over the pistachios, drizzle with the honey, then sprinkle over the basil leaves and mint. Serve immediately.

SPICED CHEWY CHOCOLATE COOKIES

I'm fussy about cookies. They need to have the right texture: usually a little crunch on the outside and a lovely chewiness on the inside. Chocolate is a must and nuts are perfectly acceptable. These don't exactly qualify as normal cookies – they are more of a meringue, being soft, chewy, sticky and so very addictive.

4 eggs whites

300g icing sugar, sifted

50g cocoa powder, sifted

good pinch of salt

150g dark chocolate chips

3 teaspoons instant espresso, dissolved
    in 3 teaspoons warm water

2 teaspoons vanilla bean paste

2 teaspoons ground cinnamon

½ teaspoon chilli powder

25g butter, melted

MAKES 20

Preheat the oven to 180ºC (160ºC fan), Gas Mark 4. Line your largest baking tray with baking paper.

Using an electric hand whisk, whisk the egg whites in a large mixing bowl until stiff peaks form.

In a separate large mixing bowl, mix the icing sugar, cocoa and salt together, then stir in the chocolate chips. Use a spatula to carefully fold in the beaten egg whites, coffee, vanilla bean paste and spices, ensuring you are folding rather than beating, to incorporate air and prevent the mixture from flattening.

As soon as you've mixed the ingredients together, brush the baking paper on the tray with the melted butter (this will make it easier to remove the baked cookies). Take heaped teaspoons of the mixture and dollop it on to the baking tray, leaving a gap of 2.5cm between each cookie – they will spread during baking. (Don't be tempted to use more than a heaped teaspoon of mixture, as they will become impossible to remove whole once baked.)

Bake for 12 minutes. The cookies will be soft when you remove them from the oven, but will crisp up as they cool. Leave on the paper to cool, then, using a fish slice, carefully remove them from the tray. This job is slightly fiddly, so be gentle when lifting them off and your patience will be rewarded. Serve immediately.

COURGETTE, ORANGE & ALMOND CAKE
WITH SWEET YOGURT FROSTING

I am rather obsessed with finding ways to pack vegetables into cakes. I would stop short at onions, but I do love making cakes with parsnips, butternut squash, beetroot and sweet potato – so why not courgettes? Their water content keeps the cake nice and moist, so they pair very well with ground almonds in this cake, which also happens to be gluten free. I just love the fragrant spike of orange zest in both the cake and the yogurt frosting.

3 large eggs

150g golden caster sugar

finely grated zest of 3 unwaxed oranges

300g ground almonds

2 large courgettes (about 300g in total), coarsely grated

150g salted butter, melted

For the frosting

150g thick Greek yogurt

50g icing sugar, sifted

finely grated zest of 1 unwaxed orange, plus extra to decorate

SERVES 10

Preheat the oven to 180°C (160°C fan), Gas Mark 4. Line a 23cm-diameter springform cake tin with baking paper.

Put the eggs and sugar into a large mixing bowl and beat together until pale and creamy. Then add the orange zest, ground almonds, courgette and, lastly, the melted butter and mix until the batter is smooth.

Pour the batter into the prepared tin. Bake for 1 hour and 20 minutes, then remove from the oven and allow to cool in the tin.

To make the frosting, combine the ingredients in a small bowl.

Carefully remove the cake from the tin and set it on a serving plate. Spread the frosting over the top surface of the cake and sprinkle with extra orange zest. The cake will keep for 2–3 days in the refrigerator, but bring to room temperature before serving.

MANGO, BLACK PEPPER & CARDAMOM POLENTA BAKE

Mangoes are among my most favourite fruits in the whole wide world. I always look forward to the brief windows in which the different varieties are in season, from Thai and Indian to Pakistani and Brazilian. In between those times canned mango purée comes into its own. It really is a gift from the heavens – it's great for cocktails, sorbets and, in this instance, a polenta traybake. A little taste of something sweet yet spicy, this is ideal topped with cooling lime-spiked yogurt.

3 large eggs

100g caster sugar

1 tablespoon vanilla bean paste

seeds from 6 cardamom pods, finely ground using a pestle and mortar

1 teaspoon freshly ground black pepper (mill it coarsely)

400g best-quality polenta (not quick-cook)

150g butter, melted

850g can sweetened mango pulp (purée)

For the lime yogurt

200g Greek yogurt

2 tablespoons icing sugar

finely grated zest of 1 unwaxed lime

1 teaspoon vanilla bean paste

SERVES 10-12

Preheat the oven to 180ºC (160ºC fan), Gas Mark 4. Line a 35 x 25cm baking tray or ovenproof dish with baking paper.

Put the eggs, sugar, vanilla bean paste, ground cardamom and pepper into a large mixing bowl and beat together. Once blended, add the polenta and melted butter and mix well, then mix in the mango purée.

Pour the mixture into the prepared baking tin and tap the tin on the counter a few times to distribute the batter evenly in the tin and smooth out the surface. Bake for 40–45 minutes, until firm. Leave to cool completely in the tin.

Combine the ingredients for the lime yogurt in a bowl until well mixed.

You can either top the entire polenta bake with the lime yogurt, or serve the yogurt on the side. Cut the polenta bake into 10–12 slices to serve.

DARK CHOCOLATE & CHERRY SHEET BAKE

Sometimes you just need a cake that is big enough to feed a crowd or to help you manage a few days' worth of stress when you clearly need a little therapy in sugary, spongy form. This is the cake for you. The cherries are frozen, so it's cheaper than using fresh cherries and means you can make the cake all year round. I suggest that, providing nobody is watching, you cut yourself a slab, lock yourself away and devour it alone.

500g pitted frozen cherries (no need to defrost them)

6 large eggs

350g caster sugar

2 teaspoons vanilla extract

2 teaspoons ground cinnamon

400g plain flour

300g unsalted butter, melted

2 teaspoons baking powder

200g dark chocolate chunks

75ml milk

SERVES 12–14

Remove the cherries from the freezer. Preheat the oven to 180°C (160°C fan), Gas Mark 4. Line a 35 x 25cm deep baking tray or ovenproof dish with baking paper.

Put the eggs and sugar into a large mixing bowl and beat together until smooth. Then beat in the vanilla extract, cinnamon, flour, melted butter and baking powder. Next, fold in the cherries and chocolate chunks, then stir in the milk to loosen the mixture a little. Mix until evenly combined.

Pour the mixture into the prepared baking tray or dish and bake for 45 minutes, or until a skewer or knife inserted into the centre comes out clean. Leave to cool in the tin before serving in squares.

RAS EL HANOUT & BUTTERMILK SWEET LOAF CAKE

WITH ROSE ICING

Ras el hanout is a highly prized blend of spices that packs an earthy punch, so you wouldn't be terribly out of line for questioning my state of mind when I first made this cake. I am pleased to report that it was a winner – and by the way, it is the rose icing that makes the cake by complementing the spiciness beautifully.

3 eggs

175g caster sugar

1 teaspoon vanilla extract

175g plain flour

150g unsalted butter, melted

1 teaspoon baking powder

1 heaped tablespoon ras el hanout

150ml buttermilk

For the topping

75g icing sugar, sifted

3 teaspoons rosewater

few dried edible rose petals, to decorate
    (optional)

SERVES 8

Preheat the oven to 180°C (160°C fan), Gas Mark 4. Line a 900g loaf tin with baking paper.

Put the eggs and sugar into a large mixing bowl and beat together until smooth. Then beat in the vanilla extract, plain flour, melted butter, baking powder and ras el hanout and mix until smooth. Lastly, add the buttermilk and incorporate well.

Pour the mixture into the prepared loaf tin and bake for 50–55 minutes, or until cooked through and a skewer or knife inserted into the centre of the cake comes out clean. Leave to cool in the tin.

To make the icing, mix the icing sugar and rosewater together in a small bowl until smooth. Once the cake has cooled, smooth the icing over the top. Sprinkle over the dried rose petals, if desired.

ORANGE, ALMOND & CARDAMOM MADELEINES

Madeleines are one of the great joys in my life and I love creating new variations. They're quick to make and small enough not to ruin a great meal, and, if you are able to have them straight from the oven, they really are spectacular. I especially like madeleines spiked with a little lemon zest, but here I combine orange zest with cardamom for a lovely, gently spiced flavour, which works a treat. These make great gifts, if you can bring yourself to give them away.

2 eggs

85g caster sugar

2 teaspoons clear honey

seeds from 4 fat cardamom pods, finely ground using a pestle and mortar

finely grated zest of 2 unwaxed oranges

90g unsalted butter, melted, plus extra for greasing

90g plain flour, plus extra for dusting

100g ground almonds

good pinch of fine sea salt

½ teaspoon baking powder

2 tablespoons milk

icing sugar, for dusting (optional)

MAKES 14–16

Put the eggs and sugar into a large mixing bowl and beat together until pale and creamy. Add the honey, ground cardamom and orange zest and mix well. Now incorporate the melted butter, followed by the flour, ground almonds, salt and baking powder. Mix until evenly combined, then stir in the milk. Cover the bowl with clingfilm and refrigerate for 1 hour (or overnight, if you wish).

Preheat the oven to 200°C (180°C fan), Gas Mark 6. Melt a little butter and, using a pastry brush, brush the recesses of a madeleine mould generously with it, then dust with a little flour, shaking off any excess.

Transfer 1 tablespoon (not too heaped) of the batter into each of the mould's recesses. Bake for 10–12 minutes, until nicely golden brown. Once cool enough to touch, remove from the moulds. Repeat with any remaining batter. Dust the madeleines with a little icing sugar, if desired, and serve immediately.

RASPBERRY & MASCARPONE NO-BAKE CHEESECAKE

I love cheesecake, but somewhere between all the complex versions out there, I lost my appetite for making it. However, this one is slightly different to some recipes, as it doesn't require baking or gelatine and doesn't set in the same way as a regular cheesecake, so the texture is softer and creamier. Even if, like me, you are not the world's most talented pastry chef, it will still be a showstopper. This cheesecake is best made and refrigerated the day before you want to serve it.

250g digestive biscuits

100g unsalted butter, melted

600g full-fat cream cheese

250g mascarpone cheese

350g icing sugar, sifted

400g raspberries

250g pomegranate seeds

SERVES 8–10

Line a 23cm springform cake tin with baking paper.

Place the biscuits in a food bag and crush with a rolling pin until finely ground, or blitz in a food processor. Transfer the crumbs to a large mixing bowl, add the melted butter and mix well. Tip the mixture into the lined baking tin and use a spatula to flatten it out into a smooth, even layer. Refrigerate for 1 hour.

Whisk together the cream cheese, mascarpone and icing sugar briefly in a large mixing bowl, just until combined, then add the raspberries and continue to whisk until evenly mixed – the mixture becomes just a little thicker once the raspberries are mixed in, and their added moisture will not make the mixture too runny. Refrigerate for 1 hour.

Remove the biscuit base and the cream cheese mixture from the refrigerator and carefully spoon the mixture over the base to fill the tin. Use a spatula to smooth out the surface until flat and even. Ensure the pomegranate seeds are dry, then add them to the top of the cheesecake in a layer so that they cover the cream cheese mixture. Refrigerate for 8 hours, or overnight.

To remove the cheesecake from the cake tin, gently place it on an overturned small bowl, then unclip and remove the tin. Carefully peel away the baking paper and slide the cheesecake on to a large plate or platter. (If the cheesecake has not set firmly enough for you to remove it cleanly from the tin, pop it into the freezer for 20 minutes.) Serve immediately.

SPICED CHOCOLATE, BLACK PEPPER & COFFEE MOUSSE

A well-made chocolate mousse has to be one of my favourite sweet treats. I love spiking chocolate with coffee – it's a wonderful flavour combination, and a little spice really does take these mousse to the next level. Serve them with thin, crisp wafers or coffee biscuits. The individual servings can be made a day or two in advance, so this really is the ideal dessert for entertaining.

150g dark chocolate (70 per cent cocoa solids), broken into small chunks

30g unsalted butter

2 heaped teaspoons best-quality instant coffee or espresso granules

1 scant teaspoon ground cinnamon

seeds from 2 fat green cardamom pods, finely ground using a pestle and mortar

2 tablespoons boiling water

3 eggs, separated

50g golden caster sugar

1 heaped teaspoon vanilla bean paste

125ml double cream

freshly ground black pepper

MAKES 4–6

Melt 100g of the chocolate in a small saucepan set over a low heat. Remove the pan from heat and stir in the butter gently until the mixture has completely melted and is smooth. Set aside to cool.

Combine the coffee, cinnamon and ground cardamom seeds in a bowl or small jug with the boiling water and stir until the coffee granules dissolve. Leave to cool.

Put the egg yolks and half the sugar into a large bowl and whisk together using an electric hand whisk until the mixture is pale. Add the cooled chocolate mixture, the cooled coffee and spice mixture, the vanilla bean paste and a generous grinding of black pepper. In a separate mixing bowl, whisk the egg whites until stiff peaks form. Set aside.

In another bowl, whisk the cream together with the remaining sugar until stiff peaks form, but be careful not to overbeat the mixture or it will become too thick. (To rescue overbeaten cream, add a little bit more cream and gently fold it in.)

Gently fold the egg whites into the chocolate mixture a heaped spoonful at a time, always folding rather than stirring, to keep the mousse light. Next, fold in the whipped cream gradually in the same way.

Divide the mixture between 4 glasses or cups or 6 espresso cups and chill in the refrigerator for a minimum of 3 hours. Just before serving, chop the remaining chocolate and sprinkle on top for decoration.

BAKLAVA BUNS

I do love a cinnamon roll and these beauties are a hybrid of that classic fused with the Eastern staple baklava. These buns are comfortingly soft and doughy with a nutty crunch, and are the ultimate crowd-pleasers for all ages. I have dispensed with the usual sweet baklava syrup and instead used honey to sweeten – add as much or as little as desired.

For the buns

350g strong bread flour, plus extra
  for dusting
7g sachet fast-action dried yeast
good pinch of fine sea salt
150g Greek yogurt
125ml lukewarm water
2–3 tablespoons olive oil

For the filling

200g unsalted butter, softened
1 heaped teaspoon ground cinnamon
125g demerara sugar
200g pistachio nuts, chopped

clear honey, to serve

MAKES 12

To make the buns, mix the flour, yeast and salt together in a large mixing bowl, then add the yogurt, the lukewarm water and olive oil and mix to a dough. It should feel supple and soft, so if the dough seems sticky, add a little more flour, or if it seems too dry, add a little extra olive oil to bring the dough together. Shape the dough into a ball, place it in the bowl and cover the bowl with a clean tea towel. Leave somewhere warm to rise for 1½ hours.

Preheat the oven to 200°C (180°C fan), Gas Mark 6. Line 2 baking sheets with baking paper.

Mix the butter with the cinnamon and set aside.

Dust a clean work surface with a little flour, then roll out the dough to a rectangular shape about 25 x 50cm. Spread the butter mixture across the surface of the dough, leaving a 2.5cm border. Scatter the sugar evenly across the buttered surface, followed by the pistachios.

Turn over the long edge of dough closest to you and start to roll it up away from you as tightly as possible. Press the end to make the dough stick. Using a very sharp knife, trim the ends, then carefully slice the dough into 12 equal rounds. Place 6 slices on each prepared baking sheet, ensuring they are spaced well apart. For best results, bake one baking sheet full of buns at a time for 18–20 minutes, or until golden brown.

Drizzle each bun with honey as desired and serve warm.

BABY BUTTERNUT BAKLAVA PIES

Although I love baklava in all its nut-filled, syrupy glory, the truth is that many Westerners find more than a piece or two a bit too sweet. So when making Middle Eastern-style desserts to suit Western tastes, these little babies were born. The addition of butternut squash gives them a wonderful texture, and I have substituted good old icing sugar for the syrup, which makes these the perfect sweet treat without sending you over the edge.

6 sheets of filo pastry, each cut into
    8 squares
icing sugar, for dusting

For the filling
200g raw cashew nuts
200g ready-roasted chopped hazelnuts
finely grated zest of 1 unwaxed orange
150g unsalted butter, melted, plus extra
    for greasing
2 teaspoons ground cinnamon, plus
    extra for dusting
300g peeled and deseeded butternut
    squash, coarsely grated
2 tablespoons clear honey
50g caster sugar

MAKES 12

Preheat the oven to 210°C (190°C fan), Gas Mark 7. Spread the cashew nuts out on a baking tray and roast for 8–10 minutes, or until golden but not too dark brown. Leave to cool, then blitz the cashews in a food processor until finely chopped.

Put the chopped cashews into a large mixing bowl with the hazelnuts, orange zest, half the melted butter, the cinnamon, butternut squash, honey and caster sugar and mix well until evenly combined.

Reduce the oven temperature to 200°C (180°C fan), Gas Mark 6.

Grease a 12-hole muffin tin. Overlap 2 squares of pastry to resemble a star, then push the star into one of the holes in the prepared muffin tin. Repeat to line each of the remaining holes.

Divide the filling mixture equally between the pastry-lined holes of the muffin tin. Press down on the filling with the back of a spoon to compress it, then flatten the surfaces.

With the remaining pastry, take 2 squares of pastry, scrunch them up, then place them on top of one of the pie fillings. Brush with some of the remaining melted butter, then fold over the pastry edges to seal the pie. Brush the tops and edges with more melted butter. Repeat with the remaining pastry squares to seal all the pies. Bake for 25 minutes, or until golden brown.

Leave the pies to cool completely in the tin. When ready to serve, dust with a little icing sugar, followed by a little cinnamon.

SPICED APPLE, THYME & HAZELNUT CAKE
WITH CINNAMON CREAM

Apples are so plentiful, and their delicate sweetness is delicious in salads. In a cake, I feel they need a nut element to complement them. This thyme-scented cake can easily be made a day in advance, as the apple keeps the cake moist. The hazelnut element complements the apple beautifully and adds a lovely crunch.

3 large eggs

225g caster sugar

2 teaspoons vanilla bean paste

1 tablespoon thyme leaves,
    finely chopped

1 heaped teaspoon ground cinnamon

1 teaspoon ground ginger

225g plain flour

1 heaped teaspoon baking powder

225g unsalted butter, melted

100g whole or halved blanched
    hazelnuts, lightly toasted in the oven
    (reserve 1 handful)

2 apples, peeled, cored and cut into
    1cm cubes

For the cinnamon cream

300ml double cream

1 heaped teaspoon ground cinnamon

3–4 tablespoons icing sugar, sifted

1 teaspoon vanilla bean paste

SERVES 8–10

Preheat the oven to 180°C (160°C fan), Gas Mark 4. Line a 23 or 24cm springform cake tin with baking paper.

Beat together the eggs, sugar, vanilla bean paste, thyme, cinnamon and ginger in a large mixing bowl, until evenly combined. Add the flour and baking powder and mix well, then beat in the melted butter until the batter is smooth. Stir in the hazelnuts, then carefully fold in the apple.

Pour the batter into the prepared cake tin and use a spatula to smooth over and flatten the surface. Now scatter over the reserved hazelnuts. Bake for 1 hour and 10 minutes, or until golden brown on top. Remove the cake from oven and leave to cool in the tin.

To make the cinnamon cream, whisk the ingredients together in a mixing bowl, using either a balloon whisk or an electric hand whisk, until the mixture is relatively stiff but still light and not overly dense. Serve the cake with a generous dollop of the cinnamon cream.

PISTACHIO, LEMON & RICOTTA CAKE

This cake is incredibly easy to make and is a real crowd pleaser. It tends to get inhaled very quickly and for good reason – the ricotta gives it a moist texture, and the lemon and pistachio are a brilliant combination. The only way this could possibly be improved would be to add a nice cup of tea and some peace and quiet.

3 large eggs

250g caster sugar

finely grated zest of 2 unwaxed lemons

2 teaspoons vanilla bean paste

250g self-raising flour

250g unsalted butter, melted

400g ricotta cheese

200g pistachio nuts, 150g finely
blitzed in a food processor
and 50g kept whole

SERVES 10–12

Preheat the oven to 180°C (160°C fan), Gas Mark 4. Line a large, deep rectangular ovenproof dish, approximately 38 x 25 x 8cm, with baking paper.

Put the eggs, sugar, lemon zest, vanilla bean paste and ricotta into a large mixing bowl and beat together until evenly combined. Beat in the flour until incorporated, then beat in the melted butter Add the ground and whole pistachios and give everything a thoroughly good mix to ensure the batter is smooth and evenly combined.

Pour the batter into the prepared dish and use a spatula to ensure it is evenly distributed and to smooth over and flatten the surface. Bake for 45 minutes, or until golden on top and a skewer or knife inserted into the centre of the cake comes out clean. Leave the cake to cool in the dish, then cut into slices to serve.

INDEX

AUTHOR'S ACKNOWLEDGEMENTS

To my agent and confidante, Martine Carter who knows me better than I know myself, and to whom I owe everything... thanks for listening to more of my problems than any good agent should ever have to, and for guiding me through the jungle that is my career with patience, truth and much kindness.

To my publisher and much-valued friend, Stephanie Jackson at Octopus Publishing who gave me my big break, puts up with my late submissions and strong-willed nature – thank you for always leading me through each project, and for your brutal honesty always letting me know exactly where I stand.

To Caroline Brown, publicity director at Octopus Publishing, and to your razor-sharp, brilliant team including Karen, Ellen, Matt & Meg who do so much hard graft to support every new book release – I am so grateful to you all for your support and guidance.

To my incredible photographer and much-loved friend, the brilliant, kind and patient Kris Kirkham. You know you are my brother-from-another-mother, and please know, no matter where I am or what I am doing, I will always be ready to share a meal with you and will have a seat waiting for you at my table. You just 'get me' and I don't even have to say anything, brother. Thanks for all your hard work, and to your assistant Eyder Rosso Goncalves, for his endless and much-appreciated cups of tea and coffee, and for always pretending to not be hungry and then eating six of everything I made.

I would like to extend a special thanks to my editor Sybella Stephens who translates 'Sabrina garble talk' into normal English ... my dear, you have the patience of a saint!

To Jonathan Christie, Jazzy 'Fizzle' Bahra, Peter Hunt and Fran Johnson for designing and creating the most beautiful books and covers every time. You have my utmost sympathies for having to work with me, but God knows, I have so much respect for you all.

A big thank you to my food stylist Laura Field, and her assistants Hilary Lester, Sonali Shah, Lizzie Evans and Sophie Pryn.

A big and very heartfelt thank you to Kevin Hawkins for all your inside wisdom and guidance whenever I've needed it, and to all the unsung heroes at Octopus Publishing. Although I rarely see you, and to those of you who I've not met, never a day goes by where I don't thank my lucky stars to have so many dedicated, hard-working people making my books the success that they are. I am incredibly fortunate to be working with you all.

A huge thank you to Alison Goff and Denise Bates at Octopus Publishing for always supporting me and making me feel more like family.

And last, but by no means least, to my friends and loved ones... those who I eat with, laugh with, cry with and who test my recipes – your love and support has, and will, continue to be the fuel that fires my creativity and gives me the confidence to keep on doing what I do. Feasting with people is something I don't take lightly; to feast with me – no matter where – means we are family. I love each and every member of my family, whether we are related or not, you have all been kind to me and taught me something valuable that I will always keep close to my heart.

And before I forget (although you know full well I could never forget), to the inimitable Mama Ghayour – the best friend, Mother and PA a girl could ask for... Thanks for always being so proud of me, no matter what... love you lots, Mugsy.

Sabrina Ghayour is an Iranian-born, self-taught home cook turned chef, cookery teacher and food writer. She made her name hosting the hugely popular 'Sabrina's Kitchen' supper club in London, specializing in Persian and Middle Eastern flavours, and went on to be named the *Observer's* Rising Star in Food. Her award-winning debut, *Persiana*, is a worldwide bestseller, and her follow-up titles, *Sirocco* and *Feasts*, have been instant bestsellers.

'The golden girl of Persian cookery' — *Observer*

www.sabrinaghayour.com

  @SabrinaGhayour

Also by Sabrina Ghayour

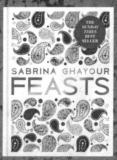

Persiana
Best Cookbook of the Year —
Observer Food Monthly Awards 2014

Sirocco
Sunday Times
No.1 Bestseller

Feasts
Sunday Times
No.1 Bestseller